FIVE COLLEGES: FIVE HISTORIES

Five Colleges: Five Histories

Edited by
Ronald Story

Published by Five Colleges, Inc., and Historic Deerfield, Inc.
Distributed by the University of Massachusetts Press

Library of Congress Cataloging-in-Publication Data
Five colleges : five histories / edited by Ronald Story.
p   cm .
Contents: Piety and play in Amherst's history / Theodore P. Greene -- Emily Dickinson's Mount Holyoke / Christopher Benfey -- The ordeal of the public sector: the University of Massachusetts / Ronald Story -- Smith College and the changing conceptions of educated women / Helen Lefkowitz Horowitz -- A brave new world: Hampshire College / Charles R. Longsworth.
ISBN 0-87023-816-7
1. Universities and colleges -- Massachusetts -- History. 2. Five Colleges, Inc. -- History. I. Story, Ronald.
LA304.5.F58   1992
378.744--dc20   92-20691   CIP
Design: Chris Clark

CONTENTS

FOREWORD

WHEN FIVE COLLEGES, INC., announced a year-long observance of the twenty-fifth anniversary of cooperation among Amherst, Hampshire, Mount Holyoke, and Smith colleges and the University of Massachusetts during the academic year 1990–1991, Historic Deerfield, Inc., thought it appropriate to salute the consortium and to take note of the museum's own five-year-old affiliation with Five Colleges. Five Colleges, Inc., quite properly looked to the present and to the future in its observances of the anniversary. Historic Deerfield, Inc., an institution devoted to Connecticut Valley history, wished to record, analyze, and reflect upon the long histories of these neighboring colleges that led to Four College cooperation in the 1950s and the founding of Hampshire College in the 1960s. Hence, *Five Colleges: Five Histories* was planned as a lecture series in which aspects of the history of each college would be presented in chronological order.

Initially, I thought that it would be easy to construct the series, knowing the strength of the history faculty in each of the colleges. To my surprise and chagrin, it wasn't easy. I telephoned friends on the various campuses for advice, looking in each case for a scholar who had pursued original research on the college history or was at least thoroughly versed in it, who would reflect on it thoughtfully and then place it in historical perspective. I was not surprised to encounter the usual sabbaticals, publication deadlines, and reluctance to assume one more responsibility during the academic year. I was dismayed to learn in some cases that the person who really knew the college history, who had done the research, who had published the article or book, had retired long ago or had died recently. There were a couple of logical choices, but putting the series together required some searching and a bit of cajoling. Although there were moments of discouragement and occasional desperation, by November of 1990 we had a full series that included both the tried and true and the inquiring. The happy result has been new research, fresh perspective, and an awakened interest in the histories of these colleges which we sometimes think have just always existed.

Having assumed chronological order, I turned first to my old friend Ted Greene, an Amherst College faculty member since 1952 and an advocate of Historic Deerfield-Five College cooperation even before the formation of Five Colleges, Inc. We both knew that he was the man to speak about Amherst College. Our conversation required only a brief and polite review of those scholars of Amherst College history who are unavailable and a slight juggling of dates to conform to Greene's travel schedule. Ted Greene is not only an Amherst College alumnus, but the son of another, and the grandson of two Amherst College graduates. He has participated actively in the history of the college and the community for many years and has written several pieces on it. Ted Greene was also very helpful, from his long experience and wide acquaintance, in suggesting contacts at the other institutions.

Mount Holyoke College offered a less clear solution. Joe Ellis, a historian and longtime dean of the faculty at Mount Holyoke, generously indicated that he would not let us down, that he would fill the breach if there was one, but encouraged us to consider others on the Mount Holyoke faculty. Most intriguing was his suggestion that we step outside the historical mold to approach the college from another angle, the experience of alumna Emily Dickinson. He told me that Chris Benfey of the English department had given a memorable baccalaureate address at Mount Holyoke and was a specialist in Emily Dickinson who could offer a fresh and stimulating perspective on Mount Holyoke in the days of founder Mary Lyon.

The University of Massachusetts offered our greatest challenge. A long conversation with Steve Nissenbaum, a member of the Advisory Committee for Historic Deerfield and of the Five College Steering Committee on the Historic Deerfield Affiliation, revealed that no one at the University was currently at work on the institution's history. He added that Ronald Story had published a book on Harvard College in the nineteenth century and suggested that I approach him about directing his attention and experience to the University's history. Ron was at first reluctant because of the press of other commitments and because of his limited prior study of UMass history, but as we talked, I sensed the emergence of a strong sense of responsibility on his part to make certain that the University of Massachusetts was represented, and represented well, in our series. He agreed to speak and in the ensuing weeks became very interested in the development of the University. As a consequence, the "Story thesis," first presented at Historic Deerfield on March 21, 1991, has had several appearances and wide currency at the University and throughout the Commonwealth.

Smith College was well prepared for our series. Mary Maples Dunn, president of Smith, a trustee of Historic Deerfield, and a historian with a strong interest in women's studies, knew that Helen Horowitz could apply her scholarship to an interpretation of Smith College's history. Her books, *Alma Mater: Design and Experience in the Women's Colleges from Their Nineteenth-Century Beginnings to the 1930s* (1984) and *Campus Life: Undergraduate Cultures from the End of the Eighteenth Century to the Present* (1987), provided a framework for the discussion of Smith College's development. She introduced to the series a material cultural perspective most appropriate to Historic Deerfield, where each year a Smith College seminar, "The Material Culture of New England, 1630-1830," is offered.

I anticipated the greatest difficulty in engaging Charles Longsworth for our series, surely not because of any lack of interest, but because I knew that the schedule of the president of Colonial Williamsburg, a museum complex many times larger than Historic Deerfield, has demands that might preclude extensive reflection on his now distant experiences in the formation of Hampshire College. Nonetheless I relied on the assumption that he must have spoken many times on the origins of Hampshire College. Chuck Longsworth accepted with alacrity, not because the lecture was already on file, but because in fact he had *never* before been asked to speak about the origins of Hampshire. His extraordinary experiences in founding the college have now been recorded!

The result is before you: a variety of approaches to a variety of experiences that make the Five College community the stimulating environment in which we happily live, teach, and learn.

Donald R. Friary
Executive Director and Secretary
Historic Deerfield, Inc.

Deerfield, Massachusetts
September 11, 1991

AMHERST COLLEGE

The Amherst College well, dug in 1820 and in service until 1911, when it was sealed as a health measure. *Courtesy of Amherst College Archives.*

Piety and Play in Amherst's History

Theodore P. Greene

Professor Emeritus of History and American Studies
Amherst College

Two months ago Don Friary told me of his plan for a series of lectures on the histories of the five colleges which form the notable consortium recently joined by Historic Deerfield. He asked me to fill the opening slot on Amherst College — and I asked *him* what he wanted me to talk *about*. He said to talk *about* forty-five minutes — and to focus on the nineteenth-century history of Amherst.

I think I have got the timing almost right. And I do propose to focus on *three separate moments* in Amherst's history, all of them before 1850.

The first will be the opening day of the new college in 1821.

The second moment will be Commencement Day fifteen years later in 1836.

Finally — after some flimflam in which the point of my title "Piety and Play in Amherst's History" will become clearer — I will conclude with extracts from a remarkable student diary describing some days in 1847.

In the process, I hope you will be able to taste some of the tangy flavor of life at Amherst College before the Civil War. And I will leave you with an unexplained paradox or puzzle about the educational quality of the college in those early decades.

ON THE THIRD WEDNESDAY OF SEPTEMBER in the year 1821, over one hundred and seventy years ago, a small group of young men assembled for the first time on Moot Hill near the town center of Amherst. With them began the history of Amherst College. What had been at first an idea, then an outpouring of support from the surrounding communities, and then one empty building on a hill, became with their arrival that mysterious blending of ideas, aspirations, architecture, and human relationships which is a college.

The total number of students enrolling on that day was forty-seven — thirty-one of them freshmen, three seniors, and among the group fifteen upperclass transfers from Williams College. These fifteen had faithfully followed the former president of Williams, Zephaniah Swift Moore, down from those western hills when — in a desire to move somewhat closer to civilization — he decided to accept the presidency of this new institution.

If the first forty-seven Amherst men were, like Amherst's present students, a select group, the principles of selection were somewhat different. No one had tried to place any statistical measure upon their verbal and mathematical aptitudes. Academically, the requirements for admission as stated in the first catalogue (a catalogue, incidentally, consisting of a single sheet printed on one side like a handbill) were simple indeed. Candidates were expected to be able to read Virgil, Cicero's orations, Sallust, and the Greek Testament as well as to display a knowledge of Latin and Greek grammar and of something described as "Vulgar Arithmetic."

In the minds of the founders of the college, of the new president, and of all *three* faculty members, however, these academic requirements were of secondary importance. The whole enterprise had begun some three years earlier not with raising an endowment fund for a learned faculty nor a capital fund for buildings, but by soliciting pledges for a charity fund which could pay all the expenses of tuition and rooming for, as the Constitution of the Charitable Fund put it, "the Classical Education of indigent young men of piety and talents, for the Christian Ministry." Despite a very severe depression which struck in 1819, the farmers, craftsmen, ministers, and merchants of several Connecticut Valley towns contributed $50,000 to the Charitable Fund and then scraped their barrels for $30,000 more in a subsequent appeal. Amherst began as a community enterprise supported by the gifts of more than 1,300 men, women, and children whose contributions ranged from fifty cents to $3,000. Though their resources were modest, their aspirations embraced the whole world. Again as the Constitution of the Charitable Fund expressed it, these gifts were made "under the conviction that the education of pious young men of the finest talents in the community is the most sure method of relieving our brethren by civilizing and evangelizing the world."

What the community and the college authorities looked for among these first forty-seven students, therefore, was not so much their academic preparation as what was called a state of "hopeful piety" and a serious interest in civilizing and evangelizing the world. Looking back some forty years later at the careers of Amherst graduates, a subsequent president of the college found the statistics, as he put it, "certainly gratifying." Of Amherst graduates from those first four classes, nearly 60 percent had gone into the ministry. Of all graduates up to 1860, over 50 percent had become ministers. And during the same period, one out of every twenty Amherst graduates had gone out to mission fields throughout the world, to Africa, Greece, the Near East, India, China, and to the islands of the Pacific (where one was eaten by cannibals).

Obviously, by modern standards, such statistics imply a rank discrimination on the basis of creed in the selection process. If this was so, it was what we now call de facto discrimination, since the charter of the college forbade any religious tests for students or faculty. From the beginning, there was no discrimination on racial grounds. In 1822, the second year of the college's existence, Edward Jones — a black student from Charleston, South Carolina — entered Amherst on a career which would take him as an Episcopal missionary to Liberia and eventually to the presidency of a college in Sierra Leone. One other possible discrimination stemming from the charity fund's initial concern for "indigent young men of piety and talents" disturbed President Moore. Before accepting the offer of his new post from the trustees, he wrote them desiring to be "assured that you will make provision for the admission of those who are *not* indigent, and who may wish to obtain a classical education in the Institution." This request caused the trustees to issue a public announcement that — providing they met the academic requirements customary at all New England colleges — Amherst would also accept for admission those who could actually afford to pay the full expenses for tuition and room rent, a sum amounting in total to ten dollars each term. The college would not discriminate against the wealthy.

In 1821, of course, it never occurred to anyone that limiting enrollment to young *men* (rich *or* poor) with no provision for young *women* was in any way discriminatory. That exclusion seemed simply a natural part of the order of things as God had created them. Only at the fiftieth anniversary of the college in 1871 did a movement first arise for the admission of women to Amherst. On that occasion this innovative step was urged by a number of alumni, including the very prominent Reverend Henry Ward Beecher — whose sister Harriet had been credited by Abraham Lincoln with starting the Civil War because of the publication of her novel *Uncle Tom's Cabin*. At this fiftieth-anniversary celebration it was announced that one of the trustees, Governor Bullock, had donated

A lithograph of Amherst College in 1824 by J. H. Bufford, after a drawing attributed to Orra White Hitchcock, wife of Edward Hitchcock, third president of Amherst College. *Courtesy of Amherst College Archives.*

funds to endow a scholarship on condition that it should be awarded to a young woman who proved her equal fitness on the entrance examinations. The proposal, however, aroused immediate fears and objections. Professor Seelye, the professor of English literature, expressed the apprehensions of many about coeducation when he explained: "Any one who has any true conceptions of the early struggles, and temptations of life, must feel great solicitude for young people, when the restraints of expediency are weak and the appetites most inflammable." Four years later, Professor Seelye himself found what seemed to him the ideal solution when he became the first president of Smith College — safely located seven miles away. One of Amherst's trustees had strongly urged Seelye to accept this post, writing him: "If you should take the presidency of this institution, you would, I think, be an important agent settling the present dispute with regard to female education and would be a means of *preventing* well-established colleges from introducing women into their existing course of study and *would thus save the community from a great amount of evil.*" After 1871, in any case, the subject did not arise seriously at Amherst for another hundred years.

Let us turn back again to the situation of those forty-seven mostly pious, frequently indigent young males who assembled on that hilltop in 1821. What kind of men were these first Amherst students, what kind of place did they come to, what kind of life did they lead? We have the firsthand recollections of one member of that initial group, who later wrote: "I remember that I was the youngest of my class. Most of my fellows were mature youths who did not appear to me youths at all, seniors in character and manlike in purpose, with an air which seemed to tell of years of yearning for the ministry, and of a brave struggle with the poverty which had kept them from this goal. They seized their late opportunity with eagerness, they were in general patient, painstaking and earnest students." (This is the kind of comment one makes on a recommendation when the student has not done very well.)

He goes on to describe the scene. Amherst then, he suggests, might well be described as "a village in the woods. Something more than a score of houses, widely separated from each other by prosperous farms, constituted Amherst center. Along two roads running north and south, were scattered small farmhouses with here and there a cross-road, blacksmith's shop or schoolhouse by way of a suburb."

"But," he continues, "the fine dwellings, public or private, of that early time had their features, whether tasteful or the reverse, greatly concealed by the wide prevalence of trees. Primal forests touched the rear of the College building; they filled up with a sea of waving branches, the great interval between the village and Hadley; towards the south, they prevailed gloriously, sending their green waves around the base and up the sides of Mt.Holyoke; to the east, they overspread the Pelham slope, and they fairly inundated vast tracts northward clear away to the lofty hills of Sunderland and Deerfield."

On Moot Hill, overlooking the village and the forests, rose the one college building (now known as South College). During the summer of 1820, this edifice had been reared in a mere ninety days of Herculean labor. It had been a true community enterprise. Men had left their farms and their shops in nearby towns to assemble on this site with contributions of bricks, granite, beams, mortar, and labor. Some slept here on the hill beside large bonfires in order to start work again with the first rays of dawn. Amherst housewives rallied to cook meals for the workers. Noah Webster and the town ministers came to lay the cornerstone, to offer prayers, speeches, and sermons. In the most eloquent of these, entitled "A Plea for a Miserable World," the Reverend David Clark proclaimed his belief that "this Institution . . . will yet become a fountain pouring forth its stream to fertilize the boundless wastes of a miserable world." He assured his audience that "any man who shall bring a beam or a rock, who shall lay a stone or drive a nail . . . shall not fail of his reward."

As a symbol of the community's dedication and zeal, the new building left nothing to be desired. As the sole facility for a college of some fifty members, however, it was a tight squeeze. By night the students studied or slept in its rooms. By day some of those rooms became classrooms or primitive laboratories. One six-foot-wide bookcase contained the college library.

Plain living and high thinking were clearly the Amherst style in those early decades. Students rose at 4:45 A.M. for morning prayers and two recitations before breakfast. The darkness of winter forced them to postpone the hour until 5:45 — but the added burdens of splitting and carrying wood for the fires in their rooms as well as breaking the ice on the college well before washing their faces prevented any undue sense of luxury from the later hour.

Nor did the curriculum afford any luxury of intellectual choice — either to students or faculty. Every course was required of every student — and in a sense almost for every faculty member. The president, for example, taught every course in senior year plus a good share of the sophomore courses. Not only the courses but even the particular book for a course was rigidly set. The catalogue did not list courses. It simply specified those books which would be read each year. Classes consisted for the most part of recitations upon the assigned portions of the standard texts. Everyone knew what a classical education meant. Everyone at Amherst knew what the saving truth was. The purpose of education was to discipline the faculties of the mind, to inculcate the great truth already revealed, and, if possible, to awaken in the student a sense of Christian grace and of Christian vocation.

The latter aims, of course, though ever present, were pursued most regularly on Sunday. Students were discouraged from doing any assigned study on the Sabbath. They were, however, expected to attend two services in the college church, where the president, occasionally assisted by the professors, did the bulk of the preaching. At intervals the college would be swept by a revival — the first occurring in 1823. Again one of those original students has left an account of this revival:

"They held early morning prayer-meetings," he recounts, "and would sometimes even in study hours, go into each others' rooms and spend a few moments in prayer, often for an unconverted roommate. At no time in the day perhaps could a person go into an entry and pass up to the fourth story without hearing the voice of prayer from some room. Prayer-meetings were held at nine o'clock in the evening in each entry, also at other times and in other places. The work of God's grace seemed to go right through the college. . . . The results have appeared in churches and the missionary fields, foreign and domestic, ever since."

CATALOGUE

OF THE

Faculty and Students

OF THE

COLLEGIATE INSTITUTION,

Amherst, Mass....March, 1822.

REV. ZEPHANIAH SWIFT MOORE, D. D. Pres. and Prof. of Divinity.

REV. GAMALIEL S. OLDS, A. M. *Professor of Mathematics and Natural Philosophy.*
JOSEPH ESTABROOK, A. M. *Professor of Languages and Librarian.*
REV. JONAS KING, A. M. *Professor of Oriental Literature.*

LUCIUS FIELD, A. B. *Tutor.*

SENIOR SOPHISTERS.

NAMES.	RESIDENCE.	ROOMS	NAMES.	RESIDENCE.	ROOMS	NAMES.	RESIDENCE.	ROOMS
Lera Fairchild,	Mendham, N. J	27	Pindar Field,	Hawley, Mass.	29	Ebenezer S. Snell,	North Brookfield, Mass.	29

JUNIOR SOPHISTERS.

NAMES.	RESIDENCE.	ROOMS	NAMES.	RESIDENCE.	ROOMS	NAMES.	RESIDENCE.	ROOMS
Paul — Allen,	Princeton, Mass.	25	David Howard,	Marlborough, Vt.	26	Elijah Paine, Jr.	Ashfield, Mass.	25
Edward Dickinson,	Amherst, Mass.	31	Theophilus Packard, Jr.	Shelburne, Mass.	32	Hiram Smith,	Westfield, Mass.	26

SOPHOMORES.

NAMES.	RESIDENCE.	ROOMS	NAMES.	RESIDENCE.	ROOMS	NAMES.	RESIDENCE.	ROOMS
Edwards A. Beach,	New Lebanon, N. Y.	10	Joseph A. Hall,	Conway, Mass.	21	Abel Packard,	Cummington, Mass.	29
Spencer F. Beard,	Stratford, Con.	15	Freeman P. Howland,	New Bedford, Mass.	23	Austin Richards,	Plainfield, Mass.	17
Charles Bentley,	Tyringham, Mass.	20	Leon — Johnson,	Plymouth, Vt.	16	Charles C. Shepard,	Little Compton, R. I.	13
Jairus Burt,	South Hampton, Mass.	20	Justin marsh,	Montague, Mass.	31	George C. Shepard,	Little Compton, R. I.	23
Iotb B. Edwards,	South Hampton, Mass.	17	Solomon Maxwell,	Lebanon, Con.	22	George Shepard,	Plainfield, Con.	28
Elisha L. Fuller,	Plainfield, Con	18	John A. Nash,	Conway, Mass.	28	Joseph K. Ware,	Conway, Mass.	28
Philander Gray,	Little Compton, R. I.	13						

FRESHMEN.

NAMES.	RESIDENCE.	ROOMS	NAMES.	RESIDENCE.	ROOMS	NAMES.	RESIDENCE.	ROOMS
Elisha G. Babcock,	Milton, Mass.	5	Ephraim Eveleth,	Princeton, Mass.	22	Charles P. Russell,	Greenfield, Mass.	6
John M. C. Bartley,	Londonderry, N. H.	12	Constant Field,	Charlemont, Mass.	30	David A. Starkweather,	Preston, Con.	14
Moses B. Bradford,	Francistown, N. H.	11	Horatio Flagg,	Wilmington, Vt.	10	Elijah D. Strong,	Amherst, Mass.	1
George Burt,	Worthington, Mass.	11	Nahum Gould,	Warwick, Mass.	3	Wright Strong,	Amherst, Mass.	1
George Burt,	Worthington, Mass.	12	Frederick W. Graves,	Amherst, Mass.	4	William M. Torrey,	Charlton, Mass.	9
Noel Campbell,	Woodbridge, N. J.	27	Homan Halbock,	Plainfield, Mass.	19	George White,	Amherst, Mass.	7
Ralph Clapp,	Southampton, Mass.	30	Moses B. Hamilton,	Palmer, Mass.	3	Walter White,	Longmeadow, Mass.	8
Lincoln Clark,	Conway, Mass.	31	Caleb S. Henry,	Brookfield, Mass.	6	Milton P. Wilder,	Princeton, Mass.	6
Robert A. Coffin,	Williamsburgh, Mass.	4	Abner J. Leavenworth,	Waterbury, Con.	14	Joel Wyman,	Westminster, Mass.	
Sylvester Cook,	Granby, Mass.		Jonathan Leavitt,	Cornish, N. H.	15			
Appleton Parkanson,	Amherst, Mass.	24	William L. Parsons,	Amherst, Mass.	8			

SENIORS, 3
JUNIORS, 6
SOPHOMORES, 19
FRESHMEN; 31

Total 59

The first printed Amherst College catalogue, with a list of all faculty and students and the students' home towns and room numbers in the lone college building on Moot Hill. *Courtesy of Amherst College Archives.*

FROM OUR PRESENT VIEWPOINT, of course, the noble aspirations of the founders of Amherst College shrink to very provincial and parochial proportions. They aimed to civilize and evangelize a miserable world by extending to that world the particular notions of civilization and of orthodox Congregationalism then current in these towns of the Connecticut River Valley. They presumed that they could and should convert all the other races and religions of the world to New England Congregationalism. The Reverend Clark's cornerstone-laying sermon had gone on to predict that because of the influence of Amherst graduates, "The heathen will be tamed to civility, and will burn their temple idols, Ethiopia will stretch out her hands unto God, the posterity of Abraham will own their allegiance to their Savior, and be again engrafted into their own olive tree, the Turk and the *Arab* will exchange the mosque and the Koran for the sanctuary and the Bible, the Tartar will pitch permanently his tent about the house of the missionary."

Closer to home a good part of the founders' zeal, in fact, stemmed from the partisan desire to combat those Unitarian heresies which Harvard College had begun to foster. Noah Webster wrote: "We do hope that this infant institution will grow up to . . . check the progress of errors which are propagated from Cambridge."

What, then, do those partisan, pious, provincial predecessors have to do with us? From our present historical perspective, from our sense of the relativity in all notions of saving truth, can we not simply dismiss these Amherst ancestors as quaint irrelevancies? I do not think so.

Do we still have anything to match the sense of *community* which in 1821 raised the funds, erected the building, and defined the purposes for this infant college? Do we have anything like the sense of *vocation* which brought those first forty-seven students to this hilltop and sent them forth throughout the world? Do we have anything to compare with the sense of *salvation* which broke forth here in periodic revivals, which led to concern for the sake of one's roommate, which persuaded the founders to take as the college motto that grand and presumptuous phrase *"Terras Irradient"* — "That they may illumine the earth"?

LET ME DESCRIBE FOR YOU another moment in Amherst's early history — a moment fifteen years later — Commencement Day at the College in 1836.

Faded newspaper clippings assure us that the day, a Wednesday, was "fair and pleasant." The date was August 24, 1836, the customary late-summer period for New England commencements. Strange as it may seem to conceive of a world where three months of summer vacation was not one of the eternal verities, this arrangement made good sense to many generations of Amherst men. A long *winter* vacation stretching from Thanksgiving on into January could be useful for "pious & indigent" young college students anxious to pick up extra cash by teaching school in rural districts.

What the town looked like on that August day in 1836 apparently depended pretty much on who was looking at it. One contemporary described it as a "neat, pretty place." To another it was simply "an ordinary country village, the streets poorly kept, the green ungraded and uncared for, no churches or other public buildings that were not eyesores … and few private houses except of the plainest New England type." About the First Congregational Church in which Commencement would be held, there was fairly general agreement. The professor of natural history and chemistry considered that this building, now known as College Hall, had been "constructed with such a sad want of taste, that it has ever been a byeword and a butt of ridicule," while another faculty member categorized it as "a cross between a dog-kennel and a cotton factory."

Though the architectural taste of its faculty may have been question-able, "the condition of the college was never more promising," as the *Boston Recorder* observed in concluding its column on the 1836

Commencement at Amherst. In the short span of fifteen years from its founding, Amherst had grown to an enrollment of 252 students, making it the second largest college in New England, second only to Yale, larger than Harvard or Dartmouth, and much larger than Williams. Some faculty members, to be sure, regretted thus losing all the educational advantages of a small college. Professor Tyler complained that "There are evils, difficulties, & dangers inevitably connected with a large College . . . which almost preclude the possibility of its realizing the idea

View of the Town of Amherst, looking west from Pelham and including the College grounds. A Pendleton lithograph after an original 1833 drawing attributed to Orra White Hitchcock. *Courtesy of Amherst College Archives.*

of a College, or doing in the best way its whole or proper work." But the trustees, meeting that week, helped to reconcile the faculty and administration to the new conditions by raising the salary of the *nine* professors to $1,000 and of the president to $1,500. Neither faculty nor trustees could foresee that within seven years the enrollment would be cut in half, much to the distress of everyone, or that it would not again reach 250 until the year 1870.

At Commencement time all 252 members of the student body were

expected to be present, and early on Commencement Day all were expected to turn out for morning prayers in Johnson Chapel. There is no reason to believe that any significant number may have overslept on this occasion, since Amherst men in 1836 were still accustomed to begin each day with morning prayers in chapel at 4:45 A.M. — and then attend one full class before breakfast. The effects of habit and piety in swelling attendance at prayers this particular morning may have been reinforced by memory of the violent scene enacted on the chapel steps immediately after Commencement Prayers the previous year. In 1835 a sophomore from Tennessee, one of a group of Southern students who referred to themselves as "the Chivalry," had turned upon a junior from New Hampshire prominent in the activities of the Anti-Slavery Society on campus. This Southern gentleman, to quote from the later faculty resolution for his expulsion, "did on the morning of last Commence-ment and immediately after prayers in the chapel, violently attack and cruelly beat a fellow-student, with a heavy cane, thus maiming his person, if not putting his life in jeopardy."

No sectional conflicts, however, marred the last devotions of the class of '36, and after breakfast the college assembled in front of chapel for the Commencement Parade. Led by a brass band and by the high sheriff of Hampshire County in his blue coat with brass buttons, the freshmen, sophomores, juniors, and seniors proceeded once around the common and up to the steps of the church promptly at nine o'clock.

As female visitors filed up into the galleries reserved exclusively for women and as the men crowded into the seats downstairs, they were handed a program of the Commencement exercises. Several of these programs survive, but *no* one can fully recapture what this long list of orations, essays, disputations, and dissertations, each with a senior's name beside it, meant to the members of the Class of 1836. In our age where it is often considered desirable to keep *down* with the Joneses, and

when the whole business of class standing is frowned upon, neither
Phi Beta Kappa, the Bond Fifteen, nor the degree with honors carries
quite the same emotional connotations which the list of Commencement
Appointments involved for our predecessors. David Riesman and others
have noted that nineteenth-century Americans looked at their world
and their lives in terms of a competitive ladder. Here in the publicly
distributed Commencement programs, the place of each senior was fixed
on a ladder which ran from the Valedictory and Salutatory Orations
down through the Philosophical Oration, the English Orations, and the
plain orations to the various dissertations, disputations, and essays,
ending finally with those forlorn graduates who received no appointment
at all. President Hitchcock in his *Reminiscences* recalled: "No one but the
valedictorian was satisfied. . . . [For most] whenever their standing is
publicly fixed, and they find it, as great multitudes always do, below what
they expected, it generally gives a terrible blow to their hopes, & they feel
as if the great object of their education had failed. . . . I have known a
worthy young man refuse to take a degree . . . because, although he had
assigned to him a first class English Oration — the word 'Philosophical'
was not prefixed to it, as he expected."

The emotional tensions generated by these Commencement listings
obviously could not always be endured in silence. The Class of 1836
won distinction and perhaps some measure of psychological release for
itself by being the first to draw up a "Mock" Commencement Program
some weeks earlier. On the cover it announced itself as "The successful
plot of a most popular college rebellion, an adoption of a way different
from that set forth by the Faculty of the College: Published and promul-
gated, and most vociferously adopted by the students of that time."
Inside were listed twenty-one items such as an "Essay by Burnap" on
"the Danger that awaits the American Nation from Mad Dogs" or
the "Dissertation by Damon," entitled simply "Woman no mystery."

Far more serious consequences were to result from these student tensions *the following year,* when a junior named Gorham rebelled against the whole system of the faculty appointing students to orations in public exercises.

This custom was observed not simply at Commencement, but at intervals during the year when the college staged public exhibitions and the faculty selected students, supposedly on the basis of competitive merit, to give a whole series of orations, essays, poems, and discourses. Students complained that the faculty appointment of students for these exhibitions was prejudiced and unfair, that the faculty displayed favoritism, that it picked students noted for their piety over other students whose intellectual merits were superior.

In 1837 as the time for the annual Junior Exhibition approached, the whole pattern of faculty control and discipline blew up in what the annals of the college describe as Gorham's Rebellion. William O. Gorham when selected to fill a particular role in this Junior Exhibition, sent the following letter:

> To the Faculty of Amherst College — Sirs:
>
> I entered College with feelings and views utterly opposed to the present system of appointments in this Institution. I have ever heartily despised and condemned the principle, and a more intimate acquaintance with it since I have been here, has rendered its effects more odious to my sense of justice. With either I can & do have no sympathy. As I cannot give countenance to this system in heart nor in tongue, I certainly will not in deed. I beg, therefore, to be freed from my appointment at the coming Exhibition and all further annoyance from this source.
>
> [Signed,] W. O. Gorham

In the face of this outrageous defiance of authority, the president (whose name was *Heman* Humphrey) called the rebel into his office and records that he "excoriated" Gorham, while describing the student's language in response as being "abusive."

The faculty thereupon prepared to put into effect the customary disciplinary procedure of the 1830s. They drew up in their own words a statement of confession and repentance which the student was expected to sign. Gorham refused to sign and his classmates supported him. Some mediators from the student body proposed that Gorham should be allowed to draw up his own confession, and the faculty finally agreed. But when the statement was received, the faculty judged it to be clearly evasive and voted for Gorham's expulsion from the college.

This faculty action triggered a revolt by the entire junior class. His classmates posted manifestoes in support of Gorham. The senior class testified to his good character. The choir went on strike and refused to take their seats in chapel.

Thus confronted and defied, all the faculty members (the full corps of nine professors plus the tutors) went to the rooms of every junior to reason with the rebels. When the full defiance of the junior class became apparent, the faculty decided that *every* junior must submit a written confession and apology for backing Gorham or be dismissed. The juniors thereupon started packing, saying they would withdraw rather than submit.

Finally at this point the faculty relented a bit. They modified the wording of the first statement they had drawn up for Gorham until he felt his conscience would allow him to sign it. His classmates then signed their own apologies. At that point, the faculty voted for a three-week holiday to allow feelings to cool — one might call it a moratorium. The infant college had drawn back from the brink of disaster.

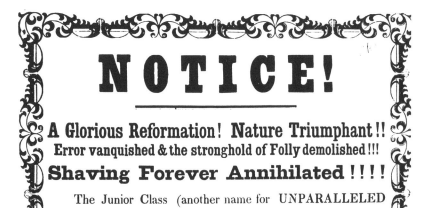

A notice by a committee of the Junior Class of 1850-51 of its intention to grow beards. *Courtesy of Amherst College Archives.*

On Commencement morning of August 24 in the previous year, however, there were no disturbances and little humor to interrupt the smooth and dignified flow of senior oratory. *Twenty-three* from a graduating class of thirty-nine members had received speaking appointments. Each piece lasted from ten to fifteen minutes. From the opening Salutatory Oration delivered wholly in Latin, through essays on "The copy-right law," orations on "The triumph of truth," and disputations over the question "Is the influence of severe or commendatory criticism more favorable to literature?," to the final Valedictory Oration on "Immortality of mental influence," the entire student body, the faculty, and a crowded throng of relatives, friends, and neighboring farmers from Hadley and Pelham sat enthralled — or at least unprotesting. At intervals of ninety minutes the feast of reason and rhetoric was temporarily interrupted by musical selections from the band or the choir. At three o'clock in the afternoon the final prayer was said, and the crowd adjourned for a cold lunch in the basement of the Church. The Amherst Class of 1836 had graduated into the hectic world of Jacksonian America.

THIS BRINGS ME FINALLY — and in conclusion — to the title of my remarks today, "Piety and Play in Amherst's History." First let me quote at some length from very perceptive observations on the intellectual life made by Richard Hofstadter (a former teacher of mine), in a book called *Anti-Intellectualism in American Life.*

"The intellectual life," he suggests, "has a certain spontaneous character and inner determination. It has also a peculiar poise of its own, which I believe is established by a balance between two basic qualities in the intellectual's attitude toward ideas — qualities that may be designated as playfulness and piety."

Hofstadter then attempts to explain what he means by these two qualities. First "piety":

"In some sense [the intellectual] lives for ideas — which means that he has a sense of dedication to the life of the mind which is very much like a religious commitment. This is not surprising, for in a very important way the role of the intellectual is inherited from the office of the cleric: it implies a special sense of the ultimate value in existence of the act of comprehension. Socrates, when he said that the unexamined life is not worth living, struck the essence of it.

"The intellectual life [takes] on a kind of primary moral significance. It is this aspect of the intellectual's feeling about ideas that I call his piety. The intellectual is engagé — he is pledged; committed, enlisted. What everyone else is willing to admit, namely, that ideas and abstractions are of signal importance in human life, he imperatively *feels.*"

But Hofstadter goes on to note that there is a danger in piety alone: "If there is anything more dangerous to the life of the mind than having no independent commitment to ideas, it is having an excess of commitment to some special and constricting idea. The effect is as observable in politics as in theology: the intellectual function can be overwhelmed by an excess of piety expended within too contracted a frame of reference."

"Piety," he says, "needs a counterpoise ... and this it has ... in the quality I would call playfulness. We speak of the play of the mind; and certainly the intellectual relishes the play of the mind for its own sake, and finds in it one of the major values in life. ... The meaning of intellectual life lies not in the possession of truth, but in the quest for new uncertainties ... the intellectual is one who turns answers into questions."

And Hofstadter concludes: "One may well ask if there is not a certain fatal contradiction between these two qualities, playfulness and piety. Certainly there is a tension between them, but it is anything but fatal; it is just one of those tensions in the human character that evoke a creative response."

Piety and playfulness — and the creative tension between them — this notion provides me the final reflections with which I would like to "play" in looking at Amherst's history.

Surely Hofstadter would argue that during the first fifty years of Amherst's existence, "the intellectual function [was] overwhelmed by an excess of piety expended within too contracted a frame of reference." Apparently this period allowed no room for playfulness with ideas, no possibility of creative tension between piety and play. The curriculum was rigidly set. In class, students did not question ideas, they recited texts. The faculty did not pursue research on unanswered questions. They preached sermons on revealed truth. The pressure for grades was unrelenting. Every student was graded on every day's recitation, and the rivalry for one's standing in class was intense. Discipline and paternalism in all aspects of life was pervasive. If ever there was an atmosphere to kill off any sense of play, any delight in ideas for their own sake, any truly spontaneous intellectual activity, that would seem to have been the atmosphere at Amherst during its first fifty years after 1821.

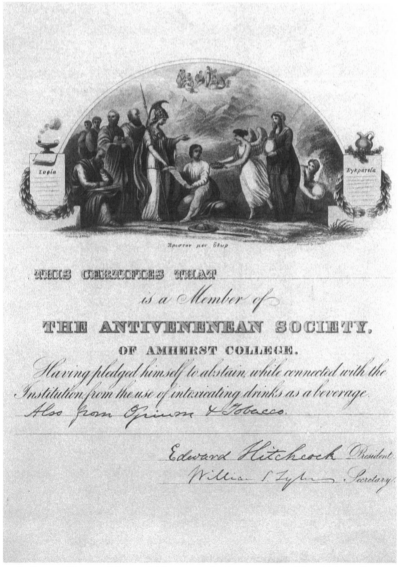

A pledge certificate of the Anti-Venenean Society, organized in 1830 to advocate abstention from "Ardent Spirit, Wine, Opium and Tobacco." *Courtesy of Amherst College Archives.*

And yet — and yet — one of the most fascinating documents from the history of any college at any time is the journal of William G. Hammond from the Amherst class of 1849. Here is a day-by-day account of a student's activities, ideas, girls, parties, emotions, triumphs, and failures. Here is conclusive evidence of a magnificently sustained tension between piety and playfulness, of a sheer delight in ideas and wit and discourse for their own sake. Let me read parts of the entries for four days in 1847 from Hammond's journal:

TUESDAY, FEB. 9 ...

EVENING. Got out lesson on Horace. Went to Psi Upsilon meeting. Afterward went down to Gay's room, drank coffee, and chatted with him. Got to my own room about 11 ½ P.M. and wrote off the first draft of a composition before 1 A.M. Subject: the great doctrine that beneath all the forms of error with which our earth abounds there lies some particle, however small, of truth. I believe this most firmly. Wrote up my journal, and to bed a little after 2 A.M.

WEDNESDAY, FEB. 10. Did not go down to breakfast. Revised part of my composition. Recitations, etc., as usual....

... After the declamation, Seelye, Poland, Lothrop, Rolfe, and I met in our room and read our compositions and criticized each other. Rolfe had a beautiful little fable, entitled "The Birth of the Dew Drop." Lothrop an essay on reformers, the best I ever heard from him. We had quite a debate on the question whether reformers were in advance of their age; ... Seelye had a good piece on the influence of belief, or as he styled it, "Our Slavery to Belief": logical and thoughtful as ever, though I have heard more elegant pieces from him. I read the essay I wrote last night. We spent a great part of the afternoon thus very pleasantly.... Our criticisms were free and carefully weighed, and many good ideas were brought out in the discussions that ensued.

We were so well pleased that we resolved to meet so again next week. . . . We are all Psi U's, all sophomores, and all room in the same entry . . . and being but few and all on an equality can join very pleasantly in any such thing.

EVENING. Waited on Miss Adams to Mr. Lord's first lecture on poetry, delivered in the rhetorical room. The high expectations I had formed were fully satisfied. . . .

After seeing Miss Adams home, went to Academia, where we had an election. Had some rare sport electioneering in a quiet way. . . . This all over, copied part of my composition, and to bed about 11 P.M.

MONDAY, JUNE 14. Studies as usual. Looked at Bridges *Conics* with dreadful anticipation. A dialogian meeting. Wrote to Mother. Called at Gridley's in the evening. [He was courting young Jennie Gridley.] A pleasant time, *of course.* Stopped at a book auction and enjoyed the fun half an hour. Feeling quite lively after my return, disguised myself, and went down and nailed up all the South College joe-doors! [I assume these were outside privies.] Read an interesting and amusing sketch in the *American Review* of "English University Life." There is something very fascinating in the associations that cluster about those old universities, with their learning and *deviltry.*

TUESDAY, JUNE 17. We had a glorious Seta meeting in my room this A.M. Lothrop and Lobdell each read a piece, and a report. The latter a capital sketch of our mountain session. Charles L. is making most marked improvement as a writer: his piece this morning, "What Will Men Think?" was the most finished and easy of all I have heard from him. Criticisms were plenty, and topics freely discussed; have rarely had a better or more profitable meeting, but we do miss Rolfe, most terribly. . . .

"After tea went to walk with Poland; coming back stopped at Gridley's, and had a most delightful hour's *tête à tête* with Jennie. Never found her so fascinating and so gracious in my life; our parting was most *tender* and she bade me remember she was my — *dear little sister.* A large portion of all this, I am aware, is a young lady's *hyperbole,* in plain language, *gammon,* yet I cannot but think there is at bottom some share of true friendship....On our way home [the next evening], talking of secret societies, Jennie G. gave me both the Psi Upsilon *and* the Alpha Delta Phi grip! Thus ended the evening's adventures!

EVER SINCE THIS JOURNAL WAS DISCOVERED and published forty years ago, Amherst's historians have tried to explain the mystery of this paradox: How — amid the apparent stultifying rigidities of the early college — could this active, independent, extracurricular delight in the play of ideas have flourished among these students?

I leave it for you as a puzzle, which may still shed some light on our continuing concern to keep alive as best we can that creative tension between piety and playfulness in the life of the mind.

MOUNT HOLYOKE COLLEGE

Detail from a drawing of Mount Holyoke Female Seminary by Catharine A. Wright, Class of 1842 and a teacher at the school from 1842 to 1845. *Courtesy of Mount Holyoke College Library/Archives.*

Emily Dickinson's Mount Holyoke

Christopher Benfey

Professor of English

Mount Holyoke College

W HEN I TOLD A FRIEND of mine that I was planning a lecture on Mount Holyoke's most famous literary alumna, she said in disbelief: "You're going to talk about Wendy Wasserstein at Deerfield?" When I clarified my intentions, she said what people always say on this subject: "But Emily Dickinson never graduated." There is a fine point hidden in this confusion, which has to do with the definition of alumna. Judging from my own nomadic education, there are people who consider you an alum if you attend a college for two days — namely, fund-raisers. And there are people who want to see a diploma — namely, prospective employers. Emily Dickinson, I think it's safe to say, never had to deal with fund-raisers or employers.

The myth about Emily Dickinson's year at Mount Holyoke Female Seminary, from 1847 to 1848, has always surrounded her reasons for leaving, never her reasons for going there in the first place. The evolution of the myth of departure is easily traced; the facts of the question of arrival are harder to come by. But they are more important for my present subject. For I am not going to use Mount Holyoke in 1847 to shed light on Emily Dickinson's youth. That has been done often and well by others. Instead, I want to use Emily Dickinson to shed light on Mount Holyoke. To put it another way, I'm concerned not with Mount Holyoke's Emily Dickinson, but with Dickinson's Mount Holyoke.

But first, let's look briefly at the myth. We tend to forget that there was a second woman in that big brick house on Main Street in Amherst, a woman who, like Emily Dickinson, never married, spending her whole life in the house where she was born — namely, Lavinia Dickinson, Emily's little sister. It was Lavinia, better known as Vinnie, who, after her sister's death, became an immediate authority on Emily Dickinson's secrets, romantic and otherwise. Vinnie had her own confident view of her sister's departure from Mount Holyoke, saying: "There were real ogres at South Hadley then."

This myth is still very much alive. My students at Mount Holyoke are always asking me *why* Emily Dickinson hated Mount Holyoke; they never ask *whether* she did. Perhaps the myth lends authority to their own gripes about college life. If Emily Dickinson hated the food, why shouldn't they? If Emily Dickinson hated her exams, why shouldn't they? And so on. And this myth, like all myths, does not simply disappear when contrary evidence is presented — on the subject of food, for example. "You have probably heard many reports of the food here," Dickinson wrote her friend Abiah Root in early November of 1847, "& if so I can tell you, that I have yet seen nothing corresponding to my ideas on that point from what I have heard. Everything is wholesome & abundant & much nicer than I should imagine could be provided for almost 300. girls."

Let us review some of the facts. Emily Dickinson came to Mount Holyoke at the age of sixteen, with excellent preparation. She had previously attended school in Amherst (where she was born in 1830) first in a one-room schoolhouse, and then at the excellent Amherst Academy, which had been founded by, among others, her grandfather and Noah Webster. After seven years at the Academy, she enrolled at Mount Holyoke Female Seminary, which had been founded ten years earlier by Mary Lyon, herself a former student at Amherst Academy. Her roommate was her older cousin, Emily Norcross. During the 1847–48 schoolyear, as in other years, there was some revivalist activity at the seminary. Mount Holyoke had a national reputation for converting its students. At the beginning of the school year students were grouped into those who professed faith (these were called professors of religion), those who had a hope, and the so-called no-hopers. Emily Dickinson, after wavering a bit, remained a no-hoper till the end, though she was not alone in this category. For a few weeks in late March and April, she had the flu, and had to spend some time recuperating in Amherst. We also know that Dickinson, like several other students, had her picture taken while at Mount Holyoke, an extraordinary piece of luck for us, since it is the only photographic image of her that has survived.

But why did Emily Dickinson want to go to Mount Holyoke Female Seminary in the first place — for there is no doubt that she did want to go. On June 26, 1846, she wrote to her friend Abiah Root:

> I am fitting to go to South Hadley Seminary [another name for Mount Holyoke], and expect if my health is good to enter that institution a year from next fall. Are you not astonished to hear such news? You cannot imagine how much I am anticipating in entering there. It has been in my thought by day, and my dreams by night, ever since I heard of South Hadley Seminary. I fear I am anticipating too much, and that some freak of fortune may overturn all my airy schemes for future happiness.

Listen to the tone of that letter: "It has been in my thought by day, and my dreams by night, ever since I heard of South Hadley Seminary." That is not the remark of a shy girl who'd prefer to stay home. It's the voice of someone who wants out, and has her reasons.

But what exactly had she heard of Mount Holyoke? We can't be sure, but we can hazard some guesses. First, she knew it was a good school academically — her father Edward Dickinson, despite his skepticism about the value of women's higher education, would have insisted on as much. She also would have known that Mount Holyoke was controversial, and had been since its founding ten years earlier. The controversy rested on several key points. First, it was a school run by women for the education of middle-class women. This raised, in conservative minds, the specter of women in general having access to higher education, and all the disruptions to family life, etc., that this would entail. Controversy also centered on the daily household chores required of the students, and the weekly practice of public confession. The first sounded to the general public like manual labor, and the second smacked of popery. Everything we know about Emily Dickinson suggests that she was drawn to controversy. Her favorite sermons, she liked to say, were about unbelief; and in a famous poem she attacked the majority for failing to see that "Much Madness is divinest Sense — / To a discerning Eye." (435)

But there is also indirect evidence that Dickinson — like many young women of sixteen or seventeen — needed to get away from her family so that she could hear herself think. Especially the voices of Edward and her brother Austin seem to have weighed on her. A palpable claustrophobia emerges in her poems about her childhood:

> They shut me up in Prose —
> As when a little Girl
> They put me in the Closet —
> Because they liked me "still" — (613)

Emily Dickinson would have had reason to believe that Mount Holyoke, if anywhere, was a place where a young woman could be heard. If the revivals at Mount Holyoke troubled her, it may have been because here again was someone telling her what to think and say.

But Dickinson was also anxious about attending Mount Holyoke, and her anxieties centered on the kind of person Mary Lyon was reputed to be, and the kind of students she was reputed to attract. "When I left home," she told her friend Abiah after a couple of weeks at Mount Holyoke, "I did not think I should find a companion or a dear friend in all the multitude. I expected to find rough & uncultivated manners, & to be sure, I have found some of that stamp, but on the whole, there is an ease & grace [&] a desire to make one another happy, which delights & at the same time, surprises me very much."

AS WE READ SUCH PASSAGES, we mustn't forget that Mary Lyon and Emily Dickinson came to South Hadley by very different routes. We tend to think of Emily Dickinson as the shy scholar and Mary Lyon as the redoubtable headmistress; but really this is in many ways a mistaken conception. The two women came from very different worlds, but it was Mary Lyon who came from the humble background, and Emily Dickinson who was to the manor born. Indeed, given the geographical proximity of Amherst and Buckland, they came from as different worlds as possible. Those who visit for the first time the Dickinson Homestead on Main Street in Amherst are often shocked at its grandeur. Maybe it's the word "homestead," which suggests a lonely outpost on the edge of civilization. Or maybe it's the myth of the New England recluse that makes us expect a hermit's hut.

But the other nickname for the Dickinson house was "The Mansion." It's a more appropriate name considering the social standing of Edward and Emily Norcross Dickinson. For Edward Dickinson was the leading lawyer in Amherst, with considerable political ambitions.

By the time his eldest daughter was six, Edward Dickinson was in the state legislature. By the time she was ten, he was in the state senate. And when she was twenty-one, he was a congressman in Washington, sharing an office with T.S. Eliot's great-uncle, of all people. Edward almost singlehandedly brought the railroad to Amherst — in recognition a locomotive was named in his honor. He pursued his career with such zeal that he sometimes seemed a bit remote to his children. He was, his daughter wrote, "too busy with his Briefs to notice what we do — He buys me many Books — but begs me not to read them — because he fears they joggle the Mind."

Everyone who thinks of the Dickinson house imagines this imposing presence in it; sometimes it's easy to forget — as Emily Dickinson seems periodically to have forgotten — that she had a mother. But the Dickinson children were proud of their father too, and they had their own political savvy. In Emily Dickinson's first letter home from Mount Holyoke, to her brother Austin, we hear the politician's daughter:

> Wont you please tell me when you answer my letter who the candidate for President is? I have been trying to find out ever since I came here & have not yet succeeded. I dont know anything more about affairs in the world, than if I was in a trance.... Has the Mexican war terminated yet & how? Are we beat? Do you know of any nation about to besiege South Hadley? If so, do inform me of it, for I would be glad of a chance to escape, if we are to be stormed. I suppose Miss Lyon would furnish us all with daggers & order us to fight for our lives, in case such perils should befall us.

While Emily Dickinson has nothing to say in her letters about the extraordinary events in Europe during the late 1840s, her reference to the Mexican War is surprising, and suggests her easy familiarity with the wider world. She was, we musn't forget, a child of privilege. If, as she later wrote, "Renunciation is a piercing virtue," we have to remember that she had something to renounce.

The contrast to Mary Lyon's background is extraordinary. For Mary Lyon was a self-made woman in just about every way — Emily Dickinson pays tribute to this self-sufficiency when she suggests that Mary Lyon would know how to defend South Hadley from an enemy attack. She was born almost two hundred years ago, on February 28, 1797. If Emily Dickinson's life seems crowded by the presence of her imposing father, Mary Lyon's childhood seemed designed to make her see the special capacities of women. Her father, a farmer in the hill town of Buckland, died when she was five years old. But the years that followed were not — as Mary Lyon remembered them — a time of hardship. On the contrary, she remembered this period as a country idyll, a frolicsome existence on what she wistfully called "that wild romantic little farm" — a phrase that inspired the many nineteenth-century paintings and drawings of Mary Lyon's birthplace. If Emily Dickinson's childhood was dominated by imposing men, Mary Lyon's was a world of strong women. The farm was run by Mary's mother Jemima, with help from the other seven children, including the eldest, her sister Electa. (The youngest was called Freelove.) Thinking of this farm, it's hard not to see an early version, a sort of nurturing dream, of the institution of women that Mary Lyon later founded.

The early history of that extraordinary institution has often been told: the years of fund-raising among a skeptical public; the first year, when the main building was not yet completed; the rumors that Mount Holyoke was a Catholic convent in disguise, or a place for training skilled servants, or worse. But by 1847, Mount Holyoke was extraordinarily successful; from more than five hundred applicants, Mary Lyon chose roughly half, and these were immediately subjected to a punishing regime of public entrance exams, three days of them. If you failed these, you were sent home, no matter how far away home was. "You cannot imagine how trying [the exams] are," Emily Dickinson told Austin, "because if we cannot go through them all in a specified time, we are sent home."

An oil portrait of Mary Lyon by Joseph Goodhue Chandler, 1844. *In the collection of the Mount Holyoke College Art Museum, South Hadley, Massachusetts. Courtesy of the Mount Holyoke College Art Museum.*

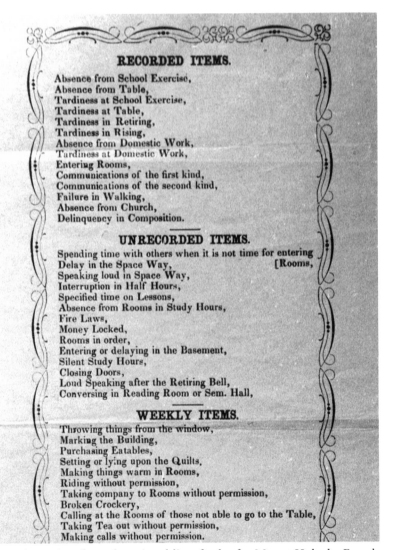

RECORDED ITEMS.

Absence from School Exercise,
Absence from Table,
Tardiness at School Exercise,
Tardiness at Table,
Tardiness in Retiring,
Tardiness in Rising,
Absence from Domestic Work,
Tardiness at Domestic Work,
Entering Rooms,
Communications of the first kind,
Communications of the second kind,
Failure in Walking,
Absence from Church,
Delinquency in Composition.

UNRECORDED ITEMS.

Spending time with others when it is not time for entering
Delay in the Space Way,   [Rooms,
Speaking loud in Space Way,
Interruption in Half Hours,
Specified time on Lessons,
Absence from Rooms in Study Hours,
Fire Laws,
Money Locked,
Rooms in order,
Entering or delaying in the Basement,
Silent Study Hours,
Closing Doors,
Loud Speaking after the Retiring Bell,
Conversing in Reading Room or Sem. Hall,

WEEKLY ITEMS.

Throwing things from the window,
Marking the Building,
Purchasing Eatables,
Setting or lying upon the Quilts,
Making things warm in Rooms,
Riding without permission,
Taking company to Rooms without permission,
Broken Crockery,
Calling at the Rooms of those not able to go to the Table,
Taking Tea out without permission,
Making calls without permission.

A sampling taken from the printed list of rules for Mount Holyoke Female Seminary in the 1840s. *Courtesy of Mount Holyoke College Library/Archives.*

The chores also turned out to be a hit, though the catalogue of 1847 still rather defensively explained: "It is no part of the design of this Seminary to teach young ladies domestic work.... Home is the proper place for the daughters of our country to be taught on this subject; and the mother is the appropriate teacher." Emily Dickinson was given an appropriate job, given her sharp-edged wit: "My domestic work," she told Abiah, "is not difficult & consists in carrying the Knives from the 1st tier of tables at morning & noon & at night washing & wiping the same quantity of Knives."

THE YEAR 1847–48 WAS MARY LYON'S LAST YEAR of full-time teaching at Mount Holyoke. She died suddenly the following year, so we must take into account that we are looking at Emily Dickinson at the beginning of her extraordinary career, and Mary Lyon at the end of her own no less extraordinary life. That they did spend a year more or less in each other's company has proved fascinating for a century, and it is the history of this fascination that I want to turn to now. We will see that each period of renewed interest in Emily Dickinson has tended to look at the relationship between Mary Lyon's institution and Emily Dickinson according to its own obsessions.

The materials concerning Emily Dickinson's year in South Hadley have been known about for a long time — most of them came to light sixty years ago or even earlier. For ease of identification, let's put them in four piles. First, there are Emily Dickinson's own extraordinary letters, twelve of which were mailed from South Hadley. Second, there is the manuscript journal (now housed in the Mount Holyoke College Archives) of day-to-day events at the seminary, which was sent off in several copies to alumnae missionaries in the Far and Middle East. In 1847–48 this informative journal was kept by two young teachers, Rebecca Fiske and Susan Tolman. (Tolman later married Cyrus Mills, and the two of them founded Mills College in California.) The third pile of sources consists of

letters and reminiscences of other students and teachers who were at
Mount Holyoke, and the fourth of miscellaneous records of visitors,
sermons, more or less reliable anecdotes, etc. You could go through the
pile on a long afternoon. And you might think that there would be some
agreement about what it all means. But it is in the nature of historical
documents to suggest different stories to different interpreters, and the
story of Emily Dickinson's year at Mount Holyoke is no exception.

Emily Dickinson died in 1886, but as everyone knows only a handful
of her poems were published during her lifetime, and none with her full
permission. Her public recognition is a phenomenon of the 1890s. The
first edition of her poems appeared in 1890, and it was so successful —
selling ten thousand copies — that a sequel followed, as well as a
selection of letters in 1894. Mabel Loomis Todd, that extraordinary
promoter of Dickinson's work, masterminded these productions. There
is much to say about Mabel Loomis Todd; she was a gifted watercolorist,
a sensitive literary critic, an insightful editor in whose debt we all remain
for having brought Dickinson's poetry to public attention. But perhaps
the strangest fact is that she never actually *saw* Emily Dickinson, even
though she was carrying on a torrid affair with Dickinson's brother
Austin during the last years of Emily Dickinson's life. Yet it was Todd's
prefaces to the poems and the letters that began to shape the public's
sense of Emily Dickinson's life and person, and what Todd emphasized
was Dickinson's reclusiveness, her renunciation of the modern world.
A prominent aspect of the marketing of the letters was Emily Dickinson's
year at Mount Holyoke. The publisher, Roberts Brothers of Boston,
clearly thought that it would boost sales to link the eccentric poet to the
celebrated founder. (In the early 1890s, Mary Lyon's name was far better
known than Emily Dickinson's.) In the brief advertisement for the book,
there is special mention of "the girlish letters dated at Mount Holyoke in
its early days ... full of allusions to Miss Lyon." Hot stuff, clearly.

And many of the early reviewers of the 1894 *Letters* took the hint, concentrating on the Mount Holyoke letters. Indeed, these letters turned out to provide the major shock of the book. Everyone was prepared — Mabel Todd had seen to it — for eccentricity, vivid nature imagery, heartfelt responses to death, and so on. But no one was ready for Emily Dickinson's chatty, gossipy, vivacious letters from Mount Holyoke. The public's idea of Dickinson was based on another myth, that of Dickinson's total renunciation of the world. She was "the New England nun," the poet who had praised "Renunciation" as a "piercing virtue."

In an editorial gloss on the 1894 *Letters,* Mabel Loomis Todd struck the new note: "Intellectual brilliancy of an individual type was already at seventeen her distinguishing characteristic, *and nothing of the recluse* was yet apparent." Todd went on to claim, on the slimmest of evidence, that Dickinson was the star of her circle of friends: "An old friend and schoolmate of Emily tells me that she was always surrounded by a group of girls at recess, to hear her strange and intensely funny stories, invented upon the spot." What was invented upon the spot, though, was probably *this* story, which is loosely based on various reminiscences by Austin and other acquaintances of Dickinson interviewed many years later.

But reviewers dutifully followed suit, expressing their surprise at what a sociable girl the fabled recluse was at Mount Holyoke. The reviewer for *The New York Times* wrote: "Not one of those South Hadley girls would have believed a prophet who should have foretold that their much-admired Emily would shut herself up while she still was a young woman and let the world take care of itself." The reviewer for the Concord (N.H.) *People and Patriot* struck a similar note: "Mount Holyoke and Emily Dickinson seem the very irony of fate: yet she expresses no dislike to that model institution ... Nothing seems to have hindered but her health. Had that not interfered, what a name would have been added to Mount Holyoke's alumnae list!" (There you can hear the accents of the fund-raiser. ...)

Dickinson was a fad of the 1890s, but she disappeared from public view, more or less, for thirty years. There was a rebirth of interest in her work during the 1920s, thanks in part to the publication of a bigger collection of her poems in 1924 and to the appearance of a rather dubious biography by her niece, Martha Dickinson Bianchi. If readers during the 1890s were drawn to the myth of the recluse who had rejected her sociable youth, the 1920s had a different version of Emily Dickinson at Mount Holyoke, as someone who had bravely rejected her religion. This new view is typified in a book published in 1930, called *The Life and Mind of Emily Dickinson.* The author was a well-known poet called Genevieve Taggard who happened to be teaching at Mount Holyoke in 1930. Taggard's chapter on Emily Dickinson at Mount Holyoke is called "The 1850 Valentine." She offers the interesting theory that Mount Holyoke was, in effect, a sort of punishment for Dickinson dreamed up by her father.

> Two young men [writes Taggard] had appeared on the horizon; they came home with Austin frequently and gained sometimes invitations to supper. Two young men were observed to be listening intently in the sitting-room below for Emily's little footstep on the stair. Emily was accordingly enrolled at Mount Holyoke Female Seminary.

And a few pages later, Taggard asserts that Edward Dickinson "had given her Seminary as he had given her a dose of nasty medicine."

Meanwhile, though, there had been taffy-pulls and F. Scott Fitzgeraldish sleigh rides with the two young men, with Emily and her cousin tucked under buffalo robes to see "one of the nicest young men in Amherst." "The wintry trips across the Notch, the shuttle back and forth between Amherst and South Hadley, rebuked Emily so thoroughly that she caught a cold and failed to shake it off." And then, almost as an afterthought, Taggard adds: "Another circumstance beset her seminary life. She was not a professing Christian." Taggard attacks the "religious coercion" practiced on Emily Dickinson, and takes pleasure in her subject's resistance to conversion. For Taggard, Mount Holyoke was a nasty little distraction from Emily Dickinson's real, that is romantic, life during the late 1840s.

Biography is often autobiography in disguise, and in Taggard's case autobiography seems to have taken over. Interestingly, Taggard had herself grown up in a fundamentalist household, where the Bible was the only book allowed in the home. After graduating from Berkeley in 1920, she arrived in New York, determined to bury her past. She became a Socialist, and was a contributing editor to the *New Masses* magazine. She also published verse that was by turns metaphysical and politically committed. But after the Crash she returned to academia. I don't know what Taggard's own two years at Mount Holyoke were like, but she had arrived there from a very different life and soon returned to it. Her book on Dickinson was widely acclaimed. She returned to New York, and in 1935 married Kenneth Durant, the American director of the Soviet news agency Tass.

ANOTHER EXHIBIT FROM THE TWENTIES can be dealt with more briefly. It is a book on the founders of five of the great northeastern colleges, including Mary Lyon. The book, entitled *Classic Shades*, is frankly elegiac, lamenting an earlier age of moral strength and character. The author is the once well-known editor and biographer who bore the wonderful name of Mark Antony de Wolfe Howe Jr. From his house on Louisburg Square, he wrote and wrote and wrote (he lived from 1864 to 1960), mainly about Boston — a history of the Boston Public Garden, a history of the Boston Symphony, a history of the Boston Tavern Club. He was an editor at that quintessentially Boston magazine, the *Atlantic Monthly*. His chapter on Mary Lyon is unabashedly admiring. Emily Dickinson enters the chapter merely to stand up to Mary Lyon, in the well-known anecdote of Emily Dickinson refusing to fast on Christmas Day.

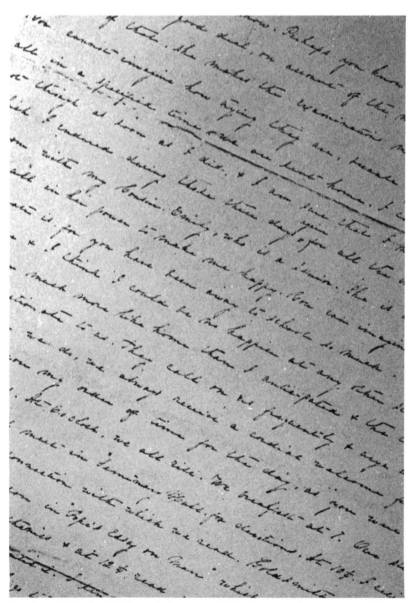

Portion of Emily Dickinson's letter to Abiah Root, written as a student at Mount Holyoke Female Seminary, November 6, 1847. *Courtesy of Mount Holyoke College Library/Archives.*

Here is Howe's account:

> On the day before Christmas Miss Lyon announced to her
> pupils that that festival would be kept as a fast, and asked all
> those who approved the plan of devoting the day to long
> hours of meditation in their rooms to signify their feeling by
> rising. With the exception of Emily Dickinson and her
> roommate the entire company rose. Aghast at this rebellion
> of spirit, Miss Lyon adddressed the girls, again seated, and
> called upon any who were still unwilling to spend Christmas
> as she had suggested to stand that all the school might see
> them. Emily Dickinson's roommate remaining glued to her
> chair, Emily stood alone. That afternoon she took the stage
> to Amherst, having provided Mount Holyoke with as good a
> Christmas story as is ever likely to be told there.

We are told by Howe's biographer that he had unusually advanced views
on the rights of women. That may be true, as long as they were New
Englanders of long standing. For toward the end of his chapter on
Mary Lyon he makes some unsettling compliments about the present —
i.e., 1920s — Mount Holyoke, and says that Mary Lyon would be
pleased with her creation. "It would please [Mary Lyon] to learn that
the College [in 1929] has not attracted either the very rich or the very
poor, especially of racial stock newly grafted on the American tree.…
The flavor of the place has accordingly a tang that is distinctively
American — not so much of the new, highly urban sort as of that older
bone-and-sinew type in the social order of which Mary Lyon herself was
an early-nineteenth-century representative." For Howe, both Dickinson
and Mary Lyon represented a "purer" America that he was afraid, from
his perch in Boston, was vanishing.

The 1890s wanted to believe that Dickinson liked Mount Holyoke,
while the 1920s wanted to believe that she hated it. A breakthrough in
scholarship was made with the appearance of Sidney McLean's article

of 1934, "Emily Dickinson at Mount Holyoke." McLean, a Mount Holyoke professor whose exhaustive research for an unfinished biography of Mary Lyon became the basis for Elizabeth Green's standard life, not only took Mary Lyon's religious life seriously, but took Emily Dickinson's spiritual struggle seriously too. Gone were the little romantic entanglements with which Taggard and Bianchi had adorned their accounts of Emily Dickinson in South Hadley. And gone was the pleasing little anecdote about Christmas, which McLean discredited thoroughly. McLean's view of Dickinson in the late 1840s became the basis for such later accounts as George Whicher's *This Was a Poet* (1938), with its probing of spiritual life in the early nineteenth century. Whicher, surprisingly, takes a stab at Emily Dickinson's Mount Holyoke roommate of all people, dismissing Emily Norcross as "an utterly colorless figure. All that we know of her is that she owned a shoe-brush and blacking. She was the kind that would." McLean, by the way, like George Whicher's wife (as well as Whicher himself, in the early 1920s), taught in the English department at Mount Holyoke. One is astonished, in leafing through the scholarship on Dickinson and Lyon, to find that so much of it had a tie to South Hadley.

But now let us hurry toward the present, pausing for a moment to ponder an observation from Thomas Johnson's perfunctory biography of 1955: "Young men and women who attended college during the 1840's were as psychologically adjusted to sporadic religious revivals as those a century later had become to recurrent world wars."

OUR LAST TWO WITNESSES are familiar names to Dickinsonians: Richard Sewall and Cynthia Griffin Wolff, Emily Dickinson's two most recent biographers. The two books are so different that it's hard to believe they're about the same person. Sewall set out to put an end to all the Dickinson myths, including the myths about Emily Dickinson hating Mount Holyoke.

His Emily Dickinson is a sly, no-nonsense Yankee — capable, bent on going her own way and writing well — the sort of person who could say, a few years before her death, "Unless we become as Rogues, we cannot enter the Kingdom of Heaven." Sewall's account of Dickinson at Mount Holyoke Female Seminary makes two major points: 1) that Emily Dickinson *liked* Mount Holyoke; and 2) that Mary Lyon and Emily Dickinson were a lot alike. Sewall notes that Mary Lyon had a sense of humor, too, and that she, like Dickinson, had hesitations about professing faith. Sewall downplays the importance of the revivals.

Indeed, for Sewall the real hero of Emily Dickinson's education was not Mary Lyon but Edward Hitchcock, the great geologist and president of Amherst who was Mary Lyon's mentor. He even refers to Mount Holyoke as "another Hitchcockian institution." (Try saying *that* in South Hadley.) Mary Lyon had two passions, Christ and chemistry; Sewall puts the emphasis on the chemistry. He argues that Dickinson left Mount Holyoke not because she was spiritually annoyed but because she was intellectually bored, having studied much of the same material at Hitchcock's Amherst Academy.

Where Sewall is sweetness and light, Cynthia Wolff is darkness and disorder. She looks at Dickinson's experience at Mount Holyoke as a sort of paradigm of the search for psychological autonomy, a clash between the individual and the group. Her account of Dickinson at Mount Holyoke is about a dark night of the soul, but it has a happy ending. For the faith Dickinson found, according to Wolff, was not faith in the Calvinist God, but faith in poetry. In 1850, her search for God temporarily closed, she wrote her friend Abiah:

> You are growing wiser than I am, and nipping in the bud fancies which I let blossom – perchance to bear no fruit, or if plucked, I may find it bitter. The shore is safer, Abiah, but I love to buffet the sea — I can count the bitter wrecks here in these pleasant waters, and hear the murmuring winds, but oh, I love the danger!

Wolff suggests, and I think she's right, that in such letters Dickinson was announcing her newfound voice; and indeed, her first poems date from roughly 1850, within a year or two after her departure from Mount Holyoke.

DID MOUNT HOLYOKE FEMALE SEMINARY help Emily Dickinson find that voice? That is a question worth pondering, and one with wide implications for us now. There were very few women's colleges in Emily Dickinson's day. There are relatively few now, and the number is shrinking. The idea of a women's college was highly controversial then. It is highly controversial now. Mary Lyon had an idea whose time had come. Some think that today that time has come and gone. Of course the pressures on women's colleges have changed. In the nineteenth century, the alternative was no higher education for women at all. The alternative today is coeducation. It is a word one never hears spoken in public on the Mount Holyoke campus today; I have heard it referred to as "the C-word." But if it isn't spoken in public, it is often whispered in private, and it is rumored that it is being talked about in high places. If coeducation should carry the day at Mount Holyoke, in ten years, or twenty years, or thirty years, it will be the end of one part of our story, that new version of the "wild romantic little farm" that Mary Lyon dreamed into existence in South Hadley. If the encounter between Mary Lyon and Emily Dickinson means anything to us, perhaps it means this question: Where can an intellectually ambitious young woman go today and listen to her own voice? Is that voice more audible among other women, or among a mixture of women and men? What would Mary Lyon say? What would Emily Dickinson say? What do we say?

Note on Sources

The best book on Mary Lyon's achievements is Elizabeth Alden Green's *Mary Lyon and Mount Holyoke: Opening the Gates* (Hanover, N.H.: University Press of New England, 1979). The standard biographies of Dickinson remain Richard Sewall's *The Life of Emily Dickinson* (New York: Farrar, Straus, 1974) and Cynthia Griffin Wolff's *Emily Dickinson* (New York: Knopf, 1986). A lucid account of Dickinson's year at Mount Holyoke, including a useful bibliography and notes, can be found in Martha Ackmann's "The Matrilineage of Emily Dickinson" (unpublished Ph.D. thesis, University of Massachusetts, 1988). Sydney R. McLean's "Emily Dickinson at Mount Holyoke" appeared in T*he New England Quarterly* 7 (March 1934): 25-42. Genevieve Taggard was completing her book on Dickinson (*The Life and Mind of Emily Dickinson* [New York: Knopf, 1930]) when she took a job at Mount Holyoke in the fall of 1929. Mark Antony de Wolfe Howe's essay on Mary Lyon is the second chapter ("Mary Lyon and Mount Holyoke") of his book *Classic Shades: Five Leaders of Learning and their Colleges* (Boston: Little, Brown, 1928), 43-77. Information on Taggard and Howe can be found in the *Dictionary of American Biography* (New York: Scribner's, 1980), in supplements four and six respectively. For reviews of Dickinson's work that appeared during the 1890s see Willis Buckingham, ed., *Emily Dickinson's Reception in the 1890s: A Documentary History* (Pittsburgh: University of Pittsburgh Press, 1989). I wish to thank Elaine Trehub of the Mount Holyoke College Archives for her help with my research.

THE UNIVERSITY OF MASSACHUSETTS

A 1969 photograph of construction on the 28-story University Library, which opened in 1973 as another legacy of the presidency of John W. Lederle. *Courtesy of Archives, University Library, University of Massachusetts/Amherst.*

The Ordeal of the Public Sector: The University of Massachusetts

Ronald Story

Professor of History
University of Massachusetts at Amherst

THE TITLE OF THIS ESSAY, "The Ordeal of the Public Sector," is a matter of timing. If I had been asked to discuss the University of Massachusetts in 1986, with the state economy doing well and the University's budget and reputation intact, I might have called this piece "The Promise of the Public Sector." Even in 1988, as budgetary storm clouds gathered amidst Governor Michael Dukakis's ill-conceived presidential gambit, I might still have managed "The Challenge of the Public Sector." As it was, the invitation to deliver the lecture on which this article is based came in 1990, during a world-class financial collapse, so "Ordeal" seemed the right word. Of course, had I known then what I know now, I'd probably be talking about "The Agony of the Public Sector," and it lessens the hurt very little to know that other public universities are experiencing agonies of their own.

I'm a historian, and this is supposed to be a historical essay. But it's difficult, if not impossible, for anyone in Amherst to forget present difficulties just now, and I'm no different. So I'll make a familiar historian's compromise and try to use history to illuminate the present. Specifically, I'll swoop through the century-and-a-quarter of University existence looking for patterns of prosperity and decline that might put our current situation in perspective. To avoid excessive gloom, I'll stay mostly with the good times. I'll also suggest why, besides biblical prophecy, these silver linings have usually hidden a cloud. I'll conclude with some comments about what sort of umbrella we should be carrying.

If you examine the University to see when certain categories — enrollment, staff, construction, operating budget — have grown rapidly and in tandem, you find four more or less distinct cycles, or phases. The first was the Founding Phase itself, which lasted from the institution's land-grant beginnings in 1863 and the admission of its first class four years later until the early 1870s, when it reached an initial enrollment peak of about 175 students, a figure not surpassed until 1890.

Phase Two was from about 1906 to 1916, when the student body and faculty both tripled in size (to some 700 and 70, respectively), the budget quadrupled (to about $700,000), and the campus had its first major building boom.

Prosperity Phase Three was from 1947 to 1954, when enrollments and staff again tripled — to 4,400 and 250 — and there was another big jump in operating funds and campus construction.

Phase Four, the most spectacular of the cycles and the one that gave "UMass" at Amherst its current look, began in 1962 and lasted for approximately a decade. At the end of this phase, there were more than three times as many students — over 20,000 — as when it started. There were also three times as many faculty — a thousand — and twice as many buildings — over 300. The operating budget was five times as large. And there were, or were about to be, new University campuses in Worcester and Boston.[1]

WHAT WERE THE KEY FEATURES of these eras of prosperity?

Phase One arose from the Morrill Act of 1862, which offered federal land to states wanting to establish colleges for instruction in agriculture, military science, and the mechanic arts, though not excluding "classical studies." States had only to add money of their own and make sure the colleges opened within five years. Justin Morrill was a Vermonter and a leading Lincoln Republican, and the Morrill Act passed Congress with the President's blessing by huge Republican majorities. The Act, and therefore the colleges it helped found, perfectly reflected the values and outlook of Lincoln Republicanism. If "the people" — in particular the middling farmers and craftsmen who comprised the base of Republican power — wanted to better themselves through their own initiative and labor, government would help them do so. "The people," in exchange, would train themselves for military and industrial service to their country in the future, just as they were providing Republican votes and Union Army soldiers in the present.

Since the Morrill Act required state action to trigger the initial land grant, there had to be political pressure in each state to ensure the action. In no state were the pressures more diverse than in Massachusetts, where organized interests had long argued for an agricultural college on the grounds that if farmers were not better educated, they could not improve the productivity of their farms enough to support themselves, and if they could not support themselves, they might leave the state or, worse, become factory workers, thereby creating a dangerous proletariat. If the college could also attack the "dissipation and indolence" of modern youth, so much the better.

But there was more involved than social control. The "opportunity" argument was very popular, especially among farmers in western Massachusetts. Besides, nineteenth-century Massachusetts obviously believed in founding colleges. Two — Tufts and Holy Cross — appeared in the 1850s, and another four — Boston University, Boston College, Worcester Polytechnic Institute, and the Massachusetts Institute of

An engraving of Massachusetts Agricultural College about 1870, showing (from left to right): Old South College, North College, Old Chemistry Building, Botanic Museum, and Durfee Plant House (foreground). *Courtesy of Archives, University Library, University of Massachusetts/Amherst.*

Technology — during the Civil War. As it turned out, this combination of regional support and institutional proliferation had significant consequences because two-thirds of the income from the Morrill land grant went to establish an agricultural college in Amherst, while the rest, for mechanical instruction, went to MIT, which became the only wholly private land-grant institution in the country. Even so, the groundwork for Massachusetts Agricultural College was laid, and with a little money from Amherst College and a little more from Amherst Town, the place opened to 56 students in 1867, and the numbers grew to 175 in 1873. Most of them were from western Massachusetts farm families.

Three points are worth noting about this Founding Phase.

First, it was partially "sponsored" by outside forces, chiefly the federal government, whose land grant constituted the "payoff" of a Republican campaign pledge: "In exchange for your blood, dollars and votes, we will give you the means to better yourself and your family by sending your sons to college."

Second, enrollments climbed quickly despite a charge for tuition, room and board of about $200 a year — over 50 percent of state per capita income. This suggests that, as Republican politicians thought, there was substantial pent-up demand for higher education of this type. Growth was "demand-driven," in other words, as well as sponsored.

Third, the state failed to subsidize the operating budget to any degree, and in fact began to castigate college spokesmen for their "annual begging" and "violation of pledges" to be self-sufficient. Since land-grant income was modest, tuition had to be the main revenue source. Inevitably, when hard times hit in the depression of the 1870s and later the mid-eighties, students stayed away because they could not pay the bills, and the college went into a slump that lasted for a generation.

GROWTH PHASE TWO coincided with the early presidency of Kenyon Butterfield, a young Michigan man whose father had farmed, worked for

Class of 1875. *(Gift of Paul W. Bunker) Courtesy of Archives, University Library, University of Massachusetts/Amherst.*

the Michigan Board of Agriculture, and taught at Michigan Agricultural College. Butterfield himself was a Michigan Aggie graduate who had done public relations work for midwestern farmers' movements and been president of the Rhode Island College of Agriculture. Butterfield had two main interests. One was agriculture, especially agricultural instruction and research, where he felt Mass Aggie trailed other agricultural colleges. The other was sociology, which he proposed to weld to agriculture by means of so-called "rural life" studies focusing on farm families and institutions as well as cultivation and crops.

To these ends Butterfield made major changes in Amherst. He hired faculty from places such as Wisconsin, Michigan, and Iowa State as well as Yale, Princeton, and Columbia, more than doubling staff size. He organized the faculty into 23 departments offering 275 courses. He then organized the departments into five divisions, including "Rural Social Science," which he himself headed. He hired the college's first accountant, dean, presidential secretary, and graduate school director, plus a new librarian and registrar. And he built a million dollars worth of buildings in ten years.

Butterfield paid his bills by increasing his budget from $150,000 in 1906 to nearly $700,000 in 1916. He did this less through higher tuition — in a couple of Butterfield years, in-state tuition was zero — than by attracting federal and state money. The federal funds came mostly from congressional programs established by turn-of-the-century farm-belt Progressives that Butterfield proved adept at tapping. The state funds (over $400,000 by 1916) came from a legislature impressed by Butterfield's rising enrollments and his aggressive rural outreach work in running summer schools for farmers and rural ministers, sponsoring school agricultural clubs, hosting state and regional agricultural conferences, organizing Polish Farmers' Day and other ethnic celebrations, arranging widespread extension work, offering correspondence courses, and founding a Federation for Rural Progress and a Rural Social Service Association.

The Agricultural Phase was clearly "leadership-driven" as the Founding Phase was not. To a striking degree, it was a reflection of Butterfield's evangelical vision of how higher education could benefit farm communities. Butterfield was *creating* demand for college more than he was *responding* to demand. He did so not by making good on a political debt, but by making "promises" about the potential of higher education to invigorate rural life.

Wintersession Class in Pomology, pruning apple trees in the Agricultural College Orchard, 1920s. *Courtesy of Archives, University Library, University of Massachusetts/Amherst.*

This helps explain Butterfield's outreach frenzy. He had to build his college on a base of Massachusetts farmers. But this population was 150,000 in 1910, down sharply from 1900 and headed lower in 1920. Given this demographic trend, Butterfield could only achieve his goals by exploiting every last ounce of support from rural Massachusetts. That he partly succeeded attests to his leadership qualities. But he succeeded only by creating a specialized college catering to a shrinking constituency. When a legislature with urban and industrial concerns balked at subsidizing agricultural educators in the 1920s and brought hiring and salaries under civil service regulations, Butterfield found himself painted into a corner, and his institution and staff with him. He resigned, with a blast at "this business of State House control," in 1924.

GROWTH PHASE THREE, our Professional Phase, coincided with the presidency of Ralph Van Meter from 1947 to 1954. Two developments paved the way. The first was World War II, which delayed educational plans and raised career expectations for thousands of men and women. This created enormous pent-up demand for career training, particularly in engineering, business administration, and teaching. And this was "effective" demand, backed by federal money from the GI bill. Since Massachusetts's private colleges lacked the capacity to meet this demand — MIT was already predominantly a national institution and would become more so — pressure built among veterans' groups, organized labor, educators, and business leaders to expand the public sector. The second development was a companion to the first. In 1931 Massachusetts Agricultural College had been renamed Massachusetts State College, signaling a step away from its roots. In 1947 the legislature changed the name of its public college to the University of Massachusetts, thereby permitting growth in kind as well as in degree.

President Van Meter took office vowing to build "a strong college of arts and science surrounded by professional schools and surmounted by a good graduate school." In fact, he put most of his energy and money where enrollment pressures were fiercest and state funds most available: new schools of engineering, business administration, and teacher training. In 1947 total enrollment was 1,700, or one student for every 500 young adults in Massachusetts. In 1954 enrollment was 4,400 — one for every 150 young adults. Of this increase of 2,700, however, only 700 came in arts and sciences. The rest (about 2,000) came in the vocational areas — engineering, business, and education, plus nursing, physical education, and agriculture — and in the small graduate school.

Three points are notable about this Professional Phase.

First, like the Founding Phase, it was partially "sponsored" by outside forces, chiefly the federal government, whose GI bill put money in the hands of prospective students by way of "paying off" the implicit

Married student housing during the postwar growth phase, 1949. *Courtesy of Archives, University Library, University of Massachusetts/Amherst.*

campaign pledge of successive New Deal war administrations: "In exchange for your blood, dollars and votes, we will give you the means to better yourself by going to college." Growth would probably have been demand-driven rather than leadership-driven anyway because of the length of the war, but the GI bill guaranteed it. Demand, in turn, determined direction: professional schools rather than arts and sciences, some professional schools rather than others.

Second, students and alumni were significant University advocates for the first time. There were, after all, more students and alumni now, including the large and insistent veterans' contingent. And UMass now attracted more students from eastern Massachusetts and sent more graduates there to live. Legislators, representing mostly eastern districts, took notice.

Third, while the state's contribution to the budget tripled, there was still substantial dependence on tuition revenues at a time when the total student bill equaled a third of Massachusetts per capita income, well above the ratio in Illinois, North Carolina, and other states with strong public universities. Moreover, not only did the legislature defeat plans for schools of law, dentistry, and pharmacy, it continued to hamstring staff recruitment with civil service restrictions, making it impossible to compete for faculty in the national market

PHASE FOUR, THE "MULTIVERSITY PHASE," began in 1962, shortly after John Lederle became president. Michigan-born, a lawyer and political science teacher with experience in state and federal government, Lederle's ambitions were immense: to build "a great public center for excellence in higher education in this region"; to create a university that would "advance the frontiers of knowledge" as well as "transmit knowledge"; to construct a "great and continuing laboratory for testing the limits of accommodation between the demands of quantity and the need for quality." "We have here," he declared, "a potential giant." Lederle's models were not just any public university, but the very best — Berkeley, Madison, and especially Ann Arbor. To reach his goal he needed not just students and facilities but faculty, especially faculty of the highest stature. To get such faculty he needed authority to hire people and pay them without state restrictions. This he won from the legislature in 1962. After that he was off to the races.

The numbers tell part of the tale. Between 1962 and 1972 enrollment increased by 280 percent to 23,000. In 1962 one of every 150 young Massachusetts adults was at UMass-Amherst; by 1972, one of every 45 was there, with more at a newly opened campus in Boston. Over 4,000 were in the graduate school; 1,000 were earning doctorates. Faculty size, meanwhile, increased by 230 percent to 1,000, the number of campus buildings by 70 percent to 300, the budget by a whopping 700 percent (450 percent after inflation) to over $100 million. With this kind of money Lederle could hire not only the number but the kind of people he wanted, and the staff to support them and their students. The average faculty salary thus rose by 90 percent (50 percent after inflation) to $15,000, and the number of support and administrative staff by 300 percent to nearly 3,000. Among the host of new Multiversity Phase initiatives, three are perhaps worth special mention because Lederle took special pride in them: a stellar university press; a public radio station; and formal cooperation among the four (eventually five) colleges of the Pioneer Valley — to which we owe, among other things, this collection of essays.

The Multiversity Phase was partially demand-driven. This was, after all, the age of the now-infamous baby boomers, when the number of Massachusetts young adults increased by half. Lederle justified his budget requests on the grounds that "young people were coming along with no place to get an education" because the "private institutions in the Commonwealth were becoming national and elitist. There was this great demand. I felt that the University of Massachusetts, being in the lead position, ought to meet that demand."

But there was clearly more to it than that. University growth vastly outstripped population increase in virtually every category. Nor was price a factor in increasing demand because total student costs remained steady at about a third of per capita state income, and there was no GI bill to reduce the pinch.

The real explanation is that this was a "leadership-driven" phase like that of 1906-1916, with another Michigander, Lederle, playing Kenyon Butterfield, developing his institution not as payment for services or to meet demand but on its promise to bring good things in the future.

An architect's rendering of the Southwest Dormitory Complex, including five 22-story towers to house 5,000 students, built during the Lederle period of the 1960s. *Courtesy of Archives, University Library, University of Massachusetts/ Amherst.*

WHAT WERE THE KEYS to Lederle's accomplishments? Some he inherited. The University designation of 1947, for instance, allowed Lederle to aspire publicly to Ann Arbor's status rather than Iowa State's, and the Professional Phase provided a critical mass of plant and people on which to build. Also, there was justification for some growth in the demographics, which projected to a 50 percent rise of young people, and some leeway to pay for it in the economics of a state that ranked ninth in per capita income but forty-eighth in tax support for public higher education.

Lederle exploited these opportunities through effective advocacy. He argued that Massachusetts should have a great public university because, as a matter of pride, we should do for our sons and daughters what Michigan and California did for theirs; because, as a matter of ambition, we should support nothing but the best; and because, as a matter of self-interest, we needed broad-based, high-quality education to fuel our economy. He also employed the rhetoric of democracy. Higher education was "an inherent part of the democratic process" and a means to develop "the talents and intelligence of every single member of society." And he argued that government could solve social problems rather than be "a mere negative policing agency."

Unlike some presidents, including Butterfield, Lederle did not generally take his message on the road to alumni and parents or chambers of commerce and service clubs, at least after the first couple of years. He worked, instead, directly with the legislature, where he testified repeatedly and at length. Lederle liked politicians and related well to them. It probably helped him that UMass students now came from all across the state, including half of them from the East. Even more helpful was the fortuitous rise to legislative power of Maurice Donahue and David Bartley, both from the Connecticut Valley and both University supporters. Lederle was also a tough, if amicable, advocate who would threaten to resign if the state rebuffed him on a vital matter. And he tried always to have four allies with him: important newspaper editors, whom he cultivated assiduously; the leadership of the League of Women Voters, which had invaluable legislative contacts; the presidents of the state's community colleges; and his own trustees, who met as often as three times a month in the late sixties in addition to testifying before the legislature.

Lastly, Lederle reached for federal dollars like no one since Butterfield. By 1970 over 10 percent of the operating budget — about $10 million — came from Washington. Lederle arrived after Sputnik and left during Vietnam. Most of his federal money therefore went to the hard sciences. Some of it helped build the elaborate Graduate Research Center and Tower. All of it facilitated his search for prestigious faculty appointments. Washington money in turn made it easier to leverage science and engineering money from the state, and so made the campus's tilt toward science and engineering more pronounced.

From the early 1970s to about 1990, the total enrollment, faculty size, and physical plant of UMass-Amherst changed relatively little. Not since the 1870s and 1880s, in fact, had these figures remained stable for so long. The operating budget tripled, to be sure, but controlled for inflation the increase was less than 100 percent over nearly twenty years. Most of the increase went for salaries or staff support, little or none for major new initiatives. State support declined as a percentage of the budget.

Since 1989 the decline in state funding has been both absolute and precipitous. At this time state funding is lower than in 1980 in real dollars, and constitutes a smaller proportion of the total budget than at any time since the early twentieth century.

Some of the resulting shortfall is being made good from federal and corporate support, which has multiplied many times since the Lederle years, and from undergraduate tuition and fees, which quadrupled in the late 1970s and again in the late 1980s. Since a year at UMass now costs

40 percent of state per capita income, the highest figure since before World War II, it may be impossible to substitute tuition for state funding much longer. And since political support in the Commonwealth has proven increasingly problematic, the University has undergone its first significant retrenchment in enrollments and faculty positions since the post-World War I period.

LEADERSHIP-DRIVEN GROWTH must rest on a proper foundation to be secure. Kenyon Butterfield, an evangelist of agrarian reform, based his Growth Phase on what was, in hindsight, a false bottom: the rural population of western Massachusetts. Are we suffering from the fact that John Lederle based his phase of prosperity, too, on a false bottom?

To the extent that institutional prosperity depends on economic prosperity, economic depressions are likely to make any foundation seem false. Other American universities, after all, are also contracting, partly because of depression-induced revenue shortfalls. But the relationship in Massachusetts has not been one to one. The depressions of the 1870s and mid-1880s hurt badly; those of the 1890s and 1930s, much less so. Recently, UMass suffered less than the Massachusetts economy in the 1970s, then prospered less in the 1980s, and now is suffering much more. It is, to some extent, our relations with the public and the legislature, rather than with the economy, that have gone awry.

This is partially a problem of ideology. The rhetoric of democracy and opportunity, of joined hands and helping hands, has underlain every phase of University prosperity, from the 1870s, with its commitment to "a liberal and practical education for the masses," to the 1960s, when Lederle tried to build "a People's University." And the reality has mostly matched the rhetoric. In 1910, two-thirds of the students were from farming or wage-earning families; in 1930, 80 percent worked to pay their bills, and in 1990 three-quarters still did. The citizenry, however, currently lacks faith in government, in opportunity, in generosity of spirit, in democratic initiative — even, it sometimes seems, in the possibility of a culture held in common or, indeed, in the efficacy of informed reason itself. In such circumstances an institution predicated on public purpose, democratic aspiration, and the life of the mind is bound to have tough sledding. The results are evident not only at the University of Massachusetts but at universities, public and private, throughout the country.

This said, it could be that John Lederle did misstep in certain crucial respects. Lederle aspired to make Amherst another Berkeley or Ann Arbor. His model, in other words, was the great public university of the day, with an eminent, research-oriented faculty and strong and influential graduate programs. But as Lederle well knew, legislators, and by extension the public, give money chiefly for undergraduate education. Berkeley and Ann Arbor were able to become premier research and graduate centers in part because they had already provided a century of large-scale, high-quality undergraduate education, from which tens of thousands of California and Michigan opinion-makers had benefited. They had, that is, already formed a mass political base that guaranteed sympathetic hearings in the Michigan and California legislatures and continued high-level funding. UMass, because it had only recently expanded, had no such alumni base on which to rely. Lederle tried to short-circuit this process by moving directly to greatness in research and graduate work. From the legislative standpoint this is a foundation of sand, unable to sustain a strong institution through difficult times. In this sense Lederle's model — the great public research and graduate university — was as inapposite as Kenyon Butterfield's.

Lederle certainly understood this dilemma in terms of selling the legislature. In the oral history he taped for the University Archives in 1975, he mentions it repeatedly.

For example: "Legislators tend to think in terms of undergraduate teaching and teaching as primary, and it's with great difficulty that you get them to appropriate directly for research. You are forced to snip this off of appropriations that were given fundamentally for other reasons."

And again: "The Legislature rarely appropriates for research per se, so that you have to squeeze and cut and work in various ways to get the state-funded support for research by squeezing it out of other things. This means fewer undergraduate teachers, teaching large classes, in order to take care of graduate students and research, and this leads you to the horns of the dilemma."

And lastly: "I have always been close to the public feeling toward universities and I knew that as far as the Legislature was concerned and as far as parents are concerned they are more interested in giving good instruction to a freshman than they are in graduate work or research. The latter they don't understand. We were obviously losing the public opinion battle because as the kids would go home, you know the usual slander of universities — You don't see a professor until you're a senior."

This dilemma helps explain something about Lederle's method of advocacy. Having no preexisting mass base, and having committed the University heavily toward research and graduate training, Lederle realized that neither the campus population nor alumni and other citizen's groups would help him much. At no time during his administration did he ever attempt to involve students or faculty in his advocacy work in any serious way. Nor did he ever really hit the rubber chicken circuit to build or energize the kind of serious University constituency, especially in eastern Massachusetts, that would make UMass an autonomous political power.

Lederle worked instead directly with the State House, depending on his skills and good relations with legislators to see him through. Since base-building takes time, and he wanted to act quickly, he felt that he had no choice. Given his time frame, he probably didn't.

Legislators bussed in from Boston by President Lederle to attend a Homecoming game in 1965. *Courtesy of Archives, University Library, University of Massachusetts/ Amherst.*

Hence his willingness to see his institution as essentially an extension of the legislature. But with his departure and the departure of his legislative contacts, the University was left with neither autonomous power base — powerful and numerous alumni — nor compelling public mission — undergraduate education — with which to leverage sufficient operating funds. And so began the drift of the 1970s that we have never wholly been able to reverse.

There seems to have been one major attempt to solve this problem: the establishment of UMass-Boston in the 1960s. Stemming as much from the legislature as from the University, this undoubtedly seemed an ideal initiative at the time, even from the standpoint of Amherst. A Boston campus focusing on undergraduate instruction would, after all, provide the visible undergraduate component and the popular eastern base that Lederle lacked, both of which he could then use to extract state funds for Amherst. In fact, it may have been a mistake for Lederle to endorse the establishment of UMass-Boston, at least in view of his expressed goals. Given the number of colleges and universities in Greater Boston, only an institution of very high reputation and quality would attract Beacon Hill's attention or enroll large numbers of future opinion-makers. Given the level of probable funding, UMass-Boston was unlikely ever to become such an institution, and in fact it has not. It may, however, have drained resources from the main campus.[2]

To repeat: Lederle wanted money to build a great university, which to him meant prominence in research and graduate work. But building such a university requires long-term, broad-based, on-going strength at the undergraduate level. Because he was in a hurry, he attempted to short-circuit the process by cultivating legislators and establishing the Boston campus. He ended up with two weak institutions instead of one strong one — and still no base. John Lederle, the greatest University leader of modern times, wound up building, like Kenyon Butterfield, on a false bottom.

WILL PROSPERITY EVER COME AGAIN? Will there be a Phase Five? If so, when and in what form?

Fat years have always, eventually, followed lean ones, and while the University has not experienced this severe a financial contraction in this century, even that doesn't preclude renewal. Substantial assets still remain, after all, including stellar faculty, a large physical plant, and an alumni body of, by now, sizable proportions. In 1991, moreover, the Amherst campus became the largest of five University of Massachusetts campuses, with a combined budget, even after the severe reductions of 1989-1992, of nearly a billion dollars and total enrollments of nearly sixty thousand students.

Even so, renewal will not come easily.

First, no Growth Phase has ever begun during a depression. While a buoyant economy does not guarantee prosperity, a down economy almost certainly precludes it.

Second, three of our four Growth Phases have rested at least partly on pent-up student demand. UMass-Amherst currently enrolls about one of every forty college-age residents in the state, not far from where Lederle left it but still the highest ratio in history; the five-campus University system enrolls one of every twenty-five college-age residents. New growth will probably require reversion to a lower ratio. That, in turn, may require some combination of more college-age people (or an expanded definition of what constitutes college-age people) and fewer choices of good colleges, neither of which is likely to happen for a while.

Third, this student demand must be effective demand — that is, the students must have money to pay. Again, tuition is historically very high relative to per capita state income. To render demand effective will require relatively lower tuition, or, more probably, more financial aid. This will, in turn, necessitate either federal action or a public-private coalition to increase state aid. Again, this is unlikely to happen for a while.

Fourth, this student demand must be substantially, if not predominantly, at the undergraduate level if the recovery is to have staying power. For political and therefore budgetary reasons, a strong research and graduate program must be sustained by a strong undergraduate program. Lederle came to understand this perfectly, even if his ambitions precluded him from acting upon it. Acting on it now will take considerable internal restructuring and long-range planning. That, too, will take time.

Fifth, we must also have support beyond the legislature if the recovery is to have staying power. This support must rest first on our alumni, especially the baccalaureates; second, on the parents and relatives of our students and alumni; and third, on other sympathetic groups and individuals. Lederle never tried to build this kind of permanent constituency, nor has anyone else. Yet it is eminently doable, and if we don't do it we will be missing an essential connection.

Sixth, no Prosperity Phase, whether demand- or leadership-driven, has ever occurred without a strong dose of democratic idealism. I'm no Pollyanna, but the record is persuasive on this point. It is no accident that we associate the 1860s with Abraham Lincoln, the 1910s with Robert La Follette and Woodrow Wilson, the 1940s with the Fair Deal, and the 1960s with the New Frontier. Until such time as citizens believe again in the legitimacy and efficacy of government and in the virtue of extending opportunity to the middle and working classes, not even economic recovery and effective undergraduate demand — not even recovery and demand coupled with leadership — will pull us wholly from the morass. And while this is partly out of our hands, we need not be utterly passive. Universities themselves, after all, have in times past helped reshape the political agenda of the age. With the right tools and the right vision, so can we.

Lastly, and most important of all, although we have never had two consecutive leadership-driven phases, neither have we faced such daunting hurdles before, at least not since 1875. I do not believe that economics or demography or even democratic idealism will now suffice. We must also have competent and visionary leadership, both on the Amherst campus and for the University system.[3] We may not attract such leaders anytime soon. Our previous leaders have largely fled the flagship, and we may have to wait awhile to get the leaders we need. When we do, we will have begun, once again, to turn the tide.

Notes

1. Basic sources for the history of the University of Massachusetts are Harold Cary, *One Hundred Years of the University of Massachusetts* (Amherst, 1962); Robert Gabrielsky, *A Research Guide to the History of the University of Massachusetts* (University History Project, Amherst, January 1989); Robert Gabrielsky, "A Time Line of University of Masachusetts History" (Typescript, University History Project, Amherst, March 1988); Robert Gabrielsky, "Construction and Protest: The Emergence of a Radical Community at the University of Massachusetts, 1960–1975" (unpublished paper, University History Project, Amherst, August 1988); John W. Lederle, *The Annual Report of the President for 1969–1970* (Amherst, 1979); "John W. Lederle, President 1960–1970," Oral History transcription, University Archives. Enrollment and other institutional data for the period after 1970 are from the annual reports of the University of Massachusetts at Amherst Office of Institutional Research and Planning. State population and income data are from the Massachusetts and United States Census Returns from 1870 to 1980, and, for the 1980s, from the New England regional reports of the United States Chamber of Commerce and the Boston Federal Reserve Bank.

2. Lederle also fell short in two areas of critical importance to public universities seeking to build autonomous institutional clout, which virtually all public universities, including Ann Arbor and Berkeley, enjoyed. One was top-flight intercollegiate sports, and especially a competitive I-A football program, which has helped flagship universities across the country sustain alumni interest and attract favorable notice among politicians and the press. The other was the right to retain student tuition, which the University relinquished, in part at Lederle's urging, around the time of his arrival. Lederle argued that even though tuition retention protected universities elsewhere during downturns and gave them a margin for building excellence in good times, such a system would lead to escalating student costs in Massachusetts, where the commitment to public education remained weak. Lederle was right to be concerned about escalating costs. He was almost certainly wrong to forego tuition retention, which not only removed a long-standing institutional cushion against recession but robbed the University of a critical resource for building autonomous political strength. The University partially compensated for its inability to keep student tuition by raising student fees, thus generating a stream of backdoor revenues that it was entitled to keep.

Another critical area where the Lederle administration might be censured is its massive construction program, which resulted in phenomenal numbers of poorly-designed, shoddily-constructed buildings. These have not only alienated countless students and employees but diverted a huge share of annual operating budgets to stopgap repairs and maintenance, thereby robbing the institution of the resources for building autonomous strength.

It is interesting to note that the shoddy construction of the Lederle era impacted most heavily on the undergraduates, who spent most of their time in or near these buildings, just as neglect of athletics made it harder to win undergraduates' enduring loyalties and the lack of a tuition retention policy made it impossible for faculty and staff to give undergraduates the attention that paying customers normally command.

3. For an outstanding analysis of the ghastly difficulties the University has had in attracting and keeping good leaders, and also the rat's nest of state politics afflicting all of Massachusetts public higher education, see Richard A. Hogarty, "The Search for a Massachusetts Chancellor: Autonomy and Politics in Higher Education," *New England Journal of Public Policy* (summer/fall 1988), 7-38; and Richard A. Hogarty, "Searching for a UMass President: Transitions and Leaderships, 1970-1991," *ibid.* (fall/winter 1991), 9-46.

SMITH COLLEGE

Awaiting the start of a festive occasion on the porch of the Students' Building. *Photo by Katherine E. McClellan. Courtesy of Smith College Archives, Smith College.*

Smith College and Changing Conceptions of Educated Women

Helen Lefkowitz Horowitz

Professor of History and American Studies
Smith College

W HEN SMITH COLLEGE OPENED IN 1875, its campus and buildings expressed a clear conception of educated womanhood. [1] As the college grew and changed, differing visions shaped its development on the land. Always, however, Smith faced a hurdle not shared by colleges for men: to offer the liberal arts to women posed a threat to the culture. Educating women beyond traditional ways has been perceived as a dangerous experiment challenging basic notions of women's nature and threatening the social order.

In the 1990s, we need to remind ourselves of the opposition to women's higher education if we are to understand the history of women's colleges. Smith and other women's colleges were designed to confront this opposition. The campus is a text upon which we can read this intention.

It is not a simple text, however, for over time different ruling images have come into play. Between its founding and the late 1930s, Smith College countered the opposition to women's higher education with four different positive conceptions of the college woman, and each shaped a portion of the campus. At the outset, the college imagined itself as the home of the feminine scholar. College students reframed the image as they promoted the all-round girl. In the early twentieth century, a new administration saw its student as a university coed, who just happened to come to Smith. And under William Allan Neilson and Ada Louise Comstock, the college reshaped itself to promote what they saw as the modern view of the Smith undergraduate, the democratic — and dating — college girl.

I. THE INITIAL DESIGN OF SMITH COLLEGE — its application of the cottage system for a women's college — was intended as a means to preserve the femininity of women subjected to the danger of the liberal arts. Its dominant conception of the educated woman was that of the feminine scholar.

To explain how this is so, I must explore the distinctive building tradition in women's higher education. The one thing that neither Smith nor other women's colleges did until the very end of the century was to follow the plan of colleges for men. By the early nineteenth century, men's colleges, whether formed piecemeal as at Yale or as a comprehensive plan as at the University of Virginia, were "academical villages." Men recited, studied, prayed, slept, and ate in a variety of structures. The buildings we would call dormitories, represented on the Yale campus by Connecticut Hall, were generally three- or four-story stretches of rooms, reached through four entries, two on a side.

Women's colleges drew on another institution, with its own distinctive history, the women's seminary, which reached its greatest influence at Mount Holyoke under Mary Lyon. In the years following the

Smith College student about 1895. *(From the album of Mary Merwin Melcher, class of 1895) Courtesy of Smith College Archives, Smith College.*

American Revolution, a new form of schooling for young men and women emerged — the academy or seminary. For female students, it offered the first hint of higher education, not a full college course, but one that in our terms straddled secondary school and college. In the early nineteenth century, the best female seminaries were those designed to train teachers. They offered training in mathematics and science, English usage, and Latin. In founding her seminary, Mary Lyon hoped both to give young women the highest education available to their sex and to change their consciousness. She sought to encourage them to bring order into their lives and to move outside the private claims of the family circle. As she put it, she would take the "daughters of fairest promise" and draw forth their talents "to give them a new direction, and to enlist them permanently in the cause of benevolence," i.e. missionary work and teaching.[2] In creating her seminary, she worked with key Amherst College professors; but never considered planning it on the pattern of Amherst or any other male college. Instead she drew on the ideas and the building tradition of the asylum.

Nineteenth-century reformers believed that if one separated those who were disordered in their minds and placed them in a structure of external order, they would internalize the rules to create an inner psychic order. This is just what Mary Lyon wanted to do. She knew the asylum well and adapted its system to a school for women. The system of Mount Holyoke Seminary thus followed the system of the asylum. The rules were strict: between the bell that awakened students at five and the one that required their lights to be off at nine, students followed a prescribed schedule of recitations, study, prayer, and housework in which they changed direction every fifteen minutes. They lived along a corridor with their teachers, and each week at "section meeting" they monitored their own behavior in a required public confessional to a specific teacher, in which they testified to how they had abided by or broken the rules.

The seminary building, erected in 1837, both expressed and enforced these rules. Everything happened in a single building, designed as an enormous house for over one hundred students and teachers. With its central entrance and stairwell, its hierarchical organization, its complete provision for living, learning, and working, Mount Holyoke had adapted the asylum to women's higher education.

In Mount Holyoke alumnae records, there is firm evidence that through the seminary system and through the power of bonding between teachers and students, Mary Lyon did change the consciousness of her pupils. To a striking degree they entered public life as teachers and missionaries. They also became internal missionaries for education, bringing the seminary system to countless other academies and to the female departments of the pioneer coeducational colleges. What happened inside the consciousness of students, however, was not necessarily observable on the outside. To most eyes, the seminary looked safe. Its rules and building protected the purity of the young women in its charge. Thus conventional daughters were sent there. The form was copied in countless schools across the country.

When, in 1861, Matthew Vassar, a Poughkeepsie brewer, followed the advice of Milo Jewett, the former head of The Judson Female Seminary, and decided to create the first real college for women, "to be to them, what Harvard and Yale are to young men," he hedged his bets by taking away on one hand what he was giving on the other. [3] He founded the first real college for women, with an undiluted liberal arts course and a full college faculty; but he linked to it the plan of governance and build-ing form of the female seminary, a quite different institution. As a result women went to college in buildings altogether different from their brothers at Yale, under supervision that their brothers would never have tolerated.

Thus, when Vassar College took form in brick and mortar, it was as an immense seminary building, designed by one of America's foremost asylum architects, James Renwick. In keeping with the newest approaches of asylum planners, Vassar College was placed on a picturesque site in the country. In a building four and five stories high and one-fifth of a mile long, the largest building in America when it was built, Renwick essentially copied the plan of Mount Holyoke Female Seminary, now for four hundred students and faculty. The central pavilion functioned as Mount Holyoke's principal floor, housing all the public spaces. One entered through ceremonial steps to find reception hall, parlor, dining room, chapel, museums for science and art, library, president's quarters, and classrooms. The male college faculty lived with their families in apartments in the end pavilions. Along the corridor, students lived with their teachers, the young female assistants of the professors. These women supervised their charges under the direction of a Lady Principal, who had the responsibility for creating and maintaining the seminary system, which attempted to control students as firmly as Mount Holyoke.

Both Vassar and Mount Holyoke were firmly established in fact and in consciousness when Hatfield, Massachusetts, resident Sophia Smith found herself late in her life, alone and with a considerable fortune, and turned to her minister, Amherst alumnus John Morton Greene, for guidance. Greene tried to interest her in his alma mater and that of his wife, Mount Holyoke Female Seminary, but she refused to visit either institution or consider leaving her money there. Greene presented her with the option of a school for the deaf or a women's college; she initially chose the former, but when another philanthropist in western Massachusetts beat her to it, she decided to endow a women's college. Greene enlisted the aid of powerful Amherst professors, and together they convinced Sophia Smith to leave the bulk of her estate for a women's college and to entrust decisions to a small group of Amherst professors and alumni.

From the outset of his conversations with Sophia Smith, John Greene was clear that Smith College should differ from Vassar and Mount Holyoke in several critical ways. Smith would not put its students into one large building, but rather build several "cottages." And instead of the isolated village or rural site, Smith would be located in the town of Northampton. Together these two features would mean that students would remain in touch with the social life of the town and would remain, as Greene put it, "free from the affected, unsocial, visionary notions which fill the minds of some who graduate at our girls' schools." [4]

When the trustees met in 1871, after Sophia Smith's death, to plan for the new college, they ratified this vision and decided that the president of Smith ought to be a man. In 1873 L. Clark Seelye agreed to be that president, confirming Amherst's influence: he was an Amherst professor and the brother of Smith trustee Julius Seelye, soon to be Amherst's president. He gave a clear articulation to the conception of Smith College and with his Amherst colleagues developed it into a plan.

At the time of Smith College's founding, reformers responsible for hospitals and asylums were questioning the proper form of institutional care. The large setting, or "congregate" system, came under attack as dangerous to the physical and mental health of its inmates. Samuel Gridley Howe, the chairman of the Board of State Charities of Massachusetts, began to understand the culture of the asylum, where inmates learned not inner order, but how to become patients. The solution that Howe found in Gheel, Belgium, was to break up the large "congregate" building and to place patients in "cottages" which simulated the family home.

Essentially, what the Amherst shapers of Smith College did was to apply this same principle to the women's college. The problem was that the women's college was breeding new dangers. The issue for Smith was less the fear of promiscuity than the fear that college women would become manly. The all-female world did not serve to protect women and conventional femininity. Instead it fostered intense female friendship and generated strong-minded women. President L. Clark Seelye had quite strong feelings on the subject of professional women, in whom "the gentle-woman is lost in the strong-minded." Quite frankly he despised them. "Is it mere prejudice," he asked, "which causes so general a feeling of aversion to some women whose energy, heroism, and ability we cannot but admire? Has not their training repressed their amiable qualities, made them bigoted, what the English would call bumptious?"[5] The solution President Seelye and his coworkers found to strong-minded women was quite wonderful in its simplicity: Educate women in college but keep them symbolically at home. Erect a central college building for instruction and surround it with cottages where the students live in familial settings. Keep them in daily contact with men as president and faculty. Build no chapel or library to encourage them to enter into the life of the town. Place students under family government as members of the town and prevent the great harm of the seminary — the creation of a separate women's culture with its dangerous emotional attachments, its visionary schemes, and its strong-minded stance toward the world.

In September 1875, when Smith College opened, it presented a bold front to the world. College Hall testified to Smith's shapers' fundamental belief in the liberal arts for women. The trustees hired a talented young Boston firm, Peabody and Stearns, to design Smith's first buildings. They planned College Hall in the design tradition of the "Old Main," the primary building of male and coeducational colleges. Accordingly they placed it on a hill, giving it a dominant place. The Victorian Gothic building that arose boldly asserted its power over the setting. It is a nervous, vital building, an assertion of muscular Christianity. Smith offered to women the liberal arts as taught at Amherst. The building for instruction therefore betrays no suggestion that it is designed for women.

Dewey House stands in sharp contrast to the main building. Its associations came not from the power of Christian learning, but from the life of Northampton through the adaption of the handsome residence of one of its most prominent early-nineteenth-century families.

College Hall in winter about 1895. *Courtesy of Smith College Archives, Smith College.*

Designed in 1827 for Charles A. Dewey, its four Ionic columns adorned a solid two-story box to which a three-story ell was added in the back. The Dewey House contained all the components of a family residence: porch, hall, parlors, dining hall, bedrooms. Nearby stood the ample house of the college president. Upon its opening the Smith College campus had every element important to the new vision: the dignified

setting for intellectual life; the domestic dwelling house; the male patri-
archal presence; placement on a central street; and no library or chapel.

Smith decided to start small. It accepted only those who could meet
the entrance requirements of a liberal arts college, creating no preparatory department, as had Vassar and Wellesley. Its initial student body of
fourteen entered in September 1875. They were greeted by the president,
a small faculty, and a director of social culture to shape their manners
and morals. In contrast to Vassar, only one rule governed their lives, the
ten o'clock rule, setting the bedtime hour of students. The daily schedule
and the students' sense of decorum established order. Students were
treated as "sensible, honorable" adults and were allowed to entertain
visitors, come and go freely, and accept invitations from friends in town.
Social freedom was part of Smith's experimental design to protect
students' femininity by keeping them within the heterosocial culture
of village life: to ensure that it was creating feminine scholars.

II.   THE SCHOLARS, HOWEVER, came to have different ideas. Students at
Smith College, and at other nondenominational women's colleges
outside the South, effectively subverted all schemes designed to keep
them within the bonds of nineteenth-century notions of feminine
behavior. It did not really matter whether you put four hundred of
them in large congregate structures separate from the world or dispersed
them in cottages integrated into a town. Either way they continued to
develop and embellish their communal world of peers, what they came
to call "The Life."

The college culture that students created at Smith and at other
women's colleges that I have studied led a fair number of them to
have notions as "affected, unsocial, [and] visionary" as that of any
Mount Holyoke student; but it did so by a different, albeit related
process. At Mount Holyoke, it was the influence of the female teacher
on the student within the structure of rules which reshaped her

Members of the class of 1895 conduct a "memorial of exams, essays, metrical travilations and the like" in Hubbard House, March 12, 1892. *Courtesy of Smith College Archives, Smith College.*

consciousness in 1837. But as early as the first years at Vassar in the late 1860s, faculty retreated to the background to become shadowy presences. There is much that one can say about this world of young women — its social divisions, inclusions, and exclusions — but for our purposes here, the most intriguing element is the way, in the bifurcated world of the late nineteenth and early twentieth centuries, that these girls taught each other to be boys. The college life that they created gave highest prestige to social roles and behaviors that the culture identified as masculine.

At issue here is not sexuality — though it may have been a contributing factor — but rather social roles, learned in the college setting. College life at Smith had the usual panoply of college organizations: newspaper, yearbook, athletic teams, drama groups, student government, honorary societies. It also contained the informal organization of student cliques, parties, and dances. The central distinction of college life in these women's colleges is that in their organizations, women compose all the officers, play all the parts. The type of student that others most admired was the one they called the "all-round girl." She was the leader — the captain of the basketball team, the president of the class, the male lead in the senior play. She had learned to wield power and to act collectively; to play as a team member and to win; to wear men's clothing and to play male dramatic roles. In a society in which gender differences attributed aggression, strength, and directness to men, the "all-round girl" of the women's college learned how to act as a man.

In the all-female dances, upperclass women took the male parts, escorting the underclass women, who had the female roles. Rather rigid rules marked upperclass students, especially seniors, off from freshmen, preserving the social distance coupled with respect. As one was initiated into the college community and moved up the hierarchy of classes, one shifted from female to male roles as one grew in power and prestige.

At the turn of the century, it was still possible for young college women to develop without embarassment highly sentimental relationships with each other that included a strong erotic component. One finds this in letters, fiction, and college poetry, some published under official college auspices. Students begin to condemn college "crushes" in the student publications; but letters and short stories suggest that female collegians accepted them as a part of the college experience. The "crush" — which is distinctive because it links to erotic feeling a power relationship — seems in fact merely an exaggeration of the basic dynamic of college life in the women's colleges of the turn of the century. The freshman admires the prestigious senior and seeks to win her

The Smith College basketball team, 1894. *Courtesy of Smith College Archives, Smith College.*

through imitation. Nothing is new about this discovery — except that in the women's college it is the way that women become socialized to play male roles.

Students re-created the social roles of men and women with their hierarchical relationships. But women took both parts, assuming masculine prerogatives as upperclass students. This encouraged the development of the forcefulness and direct stance of men rather than the tilts and smiles that marked female subordination. Designed to contain the threat to femininity posed by the liberal arts, Smith became a setting for the dramas of college life, places where women learned to act as men.

This is partially visible on the land. When Smith alumnae became established enough to begin to add to college buildings, they gave Alumnae Gymnasium, now the fitting home of the College Archives and the Sophia Smith Collection. Designed by Hartford architect William C. Brocklesby, who ultimately planned nine buildings on the Smith campus, its red brick trimmed in brownstone and its steep roofs, gables, dormers, and cupola relate it well to its companion buildings. It was here, in 1892, that women first played their own version of basketball, devised by Senda Berenson. Its vast expanse of polished floor presented space adaptable for dramatics and dances. For college-wide occasions, students transformed the gymnasium into festive settings with their private possessions.

Undergraduates began a campaign for a special building to house college life, raising the money for the Students' Building, erected in 1903. In Smith's one red brick nod to Tudor motifs, students had club rooms, a large smooth floor for dancing, and a makeshift stage for theatricals. The round-arched loggia which adorned its facade gave the proper setting for strolls during the all-female dances and the annual Promenade, the big event that brought college men on campus. Following the universal custom in the women's colleges, Smith students took up step-singing, locating it at the entry to the Students' Building.

As intriguing as are Alumnae Gymnasium and Students', they hardly measure the impact of college life on the landscape. College life did not confine itself to particular buildings. Rather students subverted the entire campus into a great stage setting for "the life." Chapel became a place for the demonstration of status, campus politicking, or the celebration of victors. The dining hall added class cheering to meals or became the scene of banquets and promenades. Students not only reshaped the spaces contained in buildings, they claimed the places in between as favorite haunts and retreats for important conversations or self-examination. College rituals which gave form to communal life cast a special aura over the landscape. Through them students claimed the college buildings as their own. On Ivy Day at Smith each class left a mark upon the land. As the settings of rituals, archways, hills, and lakes assumed a sacred quality. Thus the college campus that began as Amherst alumni's scheme for preserving femininity became transformed both in fact and in consciousness. Whatever the intentions of founders and builders, in the minds of students the buildings and landscapes of the women's colleges became the material embodiment of college life. And thus Smith, constructed so carefully to create feminine scholars, became the college of the all-round girl, and as a result created a fair share of those "strong-minded," "bumptious" women that Seelye so abhorred.

III.   SMITH COLLEGE STARTED OUT as the smallest among the women's colleges; by President Seelye's retirement in 1910, it was the largest, with almost two thousand students. All the elements that Seelye had once forsworn stood on campus: large residential halls; library; an assembly hall for chapel. They did not come by any conscious plan, but rather as a result of Seelye's growing ambition, business sense, and ability to charm philanthropists.

Smith had begun so small because it had made its entrance requirements equal to those of Amherst, limiting itself to candidates — few among women at the time — who passed the classical secondary course. Vassar and Wellesley, by contrast, had established preparatory departments to train their own students. Seelye never considered opening a preparatory school, but in 1880 he found a way to bring in more students. He created a School of Music and a School of Art. He did not integrate them into the rest of the college, but rather created largely autonomous schools with their own programs and their own diminished entrance requirements. A student needed only the equivalent of a standard high school course to qualify.

Quite unexpectedly, Winthrop Hillyer, a Northampton resident, gave $25,000 for a building for the School of Art. In 1882, the Hillyer Art Gallery opened, designed by Peabody and Stearns. When no donor appeared for a companion building for a School of Music, the college erected Music Hall to the southwest of College Hall where, as Pierce Hall, it still stands. Another variation by Peabody and Stearns on the theme of the Gothic Revival, Pierce is a solid, calm building. Only at the roofline is there any drama — a high-pitched roof, gables, smokestacks, and finials, all of which relate Pierce to its more richly decorated neighbor, College Hall.

Buttressed by the Schools of Art and Music, Smith grew quickly. Increasing numbers of students meant a need for classrooms and laboratories. In 1886, the college put Lilly Hall of Science next to the School of Music. In the twentieth century, Smith added large functional buildings for classrooms, laboratories, and communal gatherings. The early academic buildings formed an external perimeter, fronting the street. In 1900, Seelye Hall started a second tier of buildings, which filled in the center of the campus, destroying internal vistas and introducing a discordant architectural note.

With increasing numbers of students, the college erected cottage after cottage, and they grew larger and larger. The first cottages after the Dewey House — Hatfield, Washburn, and Hubbard — although of increasing size, resembled family houses in their irregular interiors and exteriors, marked by porches. So did Brocklesby's series of four cottages of the 1890s — Morris, Lawrence, Dickinson, and Tyler. Despite their size, their public rooms remain warm and domestic; and the student rooms, doubles and triples and upstairs parlors, vary in size and shape.

The original plan that Smith students use the town library grew increasingly impractical in time. Depending upon the Forbes Library, the college installed a small library within Seelye Hall. But as conflict developed between the Forbes and Smith, in 1909 Smith erected its own library, financed by Andrew Carnegie and alumnae contributions. Designed by Lord and Hewlett, the library took a classical form, a serene and calm element on an otherwise visually complicated campus. John M. Greene Hall met a need that size mandated for a place for communal gatherings and morning chapel.

When Seelye retired in 1910, the college that he turned over to his successor bore little relation to its original scheme. It had simply outgrown it. But in the years that followed, conscious planning replaced rampant growth.

From 1910 to 1917, Smith College thought "Big." At a critical moment, it harbored a midwesterner who looked at the college through the lens of a Big Ten university. In 1910 Marion LeRoy Burton came to Smith to remain until 1917, when he became president of the University of Minnesota. He brought to Smith the principles of modern college administration. He launched a succcessful endowment drive to increase faculty salaries. He encouraged faculty efforts to revamp the curriculum. He overturned existing admissions procedures to open Smith up to students from high schools. As Burton conceived of the college's student, he imagined her as a university coed, who just happened to come to Smith.

Essentially Burton devised a plan to turn Smith into a university. The existing Smith campus would become one unit of a larger institution composed of colleges either of social science, art, music, and drama or of a nonspecialized nature, following the English model. To enable this he sought to expand the campus by acquiring more land. And he hired landscape architect and city planner John Nolan to evaluate the existing campus and devise a scheme. When Burton returned to the Midwest, his university plan went with him. He had set in motion, however, the processes of land acquisition and planning that would be turned to quite different purposes.

Smith College houses about 1887 (left to right): Hubbard, Washburn, Hatfield, Dewey. *Photo by E.A. Record. Courtesy of Smith College Archives, Smith College.*

IV. IN 1912 BURTON HAD BROUGHT ADA LOUISE COMSTOCK, a Smith alumna, as his dean. She had been dean of women at the University of Minnesota since 1907. As she surveyed the campus, she found herself disturbed by what had happened at Smith: increasing divisions had emerged between students, divisions that were intensified by the growth of off-campus housing. The college had admitted more students than there were college rooms. By the turn of the century one-half of Smith's student body, including the upper classes, lived in rooming houses.

While the college regulated these off-campus boardinghouses, the conditions they offered varied considerably. For the poorest students, they could be less expensive than the dormitory. For richer, they became a way of confirming social prestige and living in luxury. One joined some of them through a network of friends. When a group of students set up their own house, renting it and hiring a matron, they created an "invitation house" which chose the next year's occupants through a formal vote. While never receiving the name "sorority," White Lodge and Delta Sigma linked residence and social selection in much the same manner as did the Greek societies on coeducational campuses. Smith had gotten something of a Gold Coast as well. De Witt Smith, a speculative builder from New York and a Yale man, erected the Plymouth, a handsome Richardsonian-Romanesque apartment house adjacent to the campus. With its grand marble-encased public rooms, expensive suites for sixty-four students, gymnasium and swimming pool, and dining room equipped with a stage, the Plymouth created a new level of extravagance and exclusion among college women. Unwittingly Smith's residence policy had allowed students to sort themselves out economically and socially: cliques embedded themselves in residential groups, giving spatial form to distinctions within the student body.

This was disturbing to Comstock. She believed strongly in the ideal of Smith democracy. "Of all the diguises which the human spirit assumes none is so complete as that embodied in circumstances of living."

Inhibitions springing from economic differences existed in the outside world, but "in college . . . we have our chance to see what the human spirit can do when unhampered either by deprivation or by excess."[6] In her campaign to democratize Smith College, Comstock was joined by William Allan Neilson, who followed Burton as president. Neilson's primary concern was with intellectual quality, not with campus expansion; and he only accepted the presidency once the trustees tabled plans for a women's university. He came with the hopes of remaining a scholar: he quickly became a master fund-raiser. His Scottish commitment to the principles of equality required him to seek funds to build residential halls. After major campaigns, in 1934 he announced that Smith at last could house its students.

While the college received the bequest of the Capen School and purchased private dormitories, to house over a thousand additional students it had to undertake major building. The result for Smith was dramatic: the Quadrangles on Allen Field, ten residential halls designed by the Boston architect John W. Ames and his collaborators Edwin Sherrill Dodge and Karl S. Putnam. Each dormitory was named in honor of a distinguished member of the Smith community, including Ellen Emerson, Martha Wilson, Laura Scales, Franklin King, and Comstock.

With the Quadrangles, Smith entered the mainstream of collegiate architecture — in its red brick Georgian variant. In many ways Smith's complex of residential halls looks like the new Harvard houses which rose in the same period on the Charles River. Initially, Ames's scheme seemed to the trustees too like industrial buildings. As a result, Ames enlivened the regularity and symmetry of the four-story structures by generous use of white trim for windows, stringcourses, and cupolas, by dormer windows and tall red brick chimneys, by round-arched loggias and white service buildings. In their associations, the Quadrangles assert the dignity of college life.

Yet in their interiors, the Quadrangles quietly continued the separate building tradition of women's dormitories. At Harvard the houses had suites of connecting undergraduate rooms, each sharing bathroom and living room, designed to foster male friendship and camaraderie. In the 1920s and 1930s, Smith and other women's colleges became fearful of female intimacy. The dormitories reflect this fear. They lost the informal, irregular space of the cottages, with their doubles, triples, and suites. Instead they put students in single identical Spartan cubicles on both sides of a long corridor. Such interiors were intended to discourage socializing upstairs away from adult eyes. Downstairs, elegant public rooms, designed by alumnae who were professional interior decorators, allowed gatherings that could be monitored and provided luxurious spaces in which male guests could be received.

The building group allowed Smith to create a planned, regular space in keeping with Beaux Arts principles then governing campus design. The other side of this is that the Quadrangles created a world different from that of the rest of the campus and of the town. Brick walls front the street; courtyards create an inner enclosed space. The cottages and boardinghouses had interpersed students both on campus and in the town. With the Quadrangles, Smith set half of its students off in their own residential quarter and away from Northampton. Their construction signaled the supplanting of Smith's original vision of the feminine collegian by Neilson and Comstock's hope for a democratic, heterosexual college girl.

THE CAMPUS OF SMITH COLLEGE IS A TEXT that dramatizes significant episodes in the past of Smith College. Even in its outlines, the narrative of college building at Smith, from its founding until the late 1930s, is richly complex. Differing conceptions of educated womanhood offered alternative patterns for building. Four visions of the ideal Smith

Mandelle Quadrangle about 1930. *Photo by Richard Averill Smith, Woodside, N.Y. Courtesy of Smith College Archives, Smith College.*

student are embedded in bricks and mortar: the feminine scholar; the all-round girl; the university coed, who just happened to come to Smith; and the democratic and dating college girl. Implicit is a dialectical understanding. Each vision is posed in part as an answer to a question grounded in the opposition to women's higher education.

Buildings always have unintended consequences. Moreover, the history of Smith's building intentions is not the whole history of Smith. Looking at Smith's structures, however, affords a window for looking into Smith's design that tells us much about the hopes and fears that offering women the liberal arts has evoked.

Today, the design of the college, with all its tensions and contradictions, does not determine the present. It does, however, establish part of the ground of dialogue, debate, and choice. As the decisions that will shape future campus plans are posed, there are echoes of the past, as well as new conceptions of educated womanhood that the past could not begin to envision.

Notes

1. This article abridges sections of my *Alma Mater: Design and Experience in the Women's Colleges from Their Nineteenth-Century Beginnings to the 1930s* (New York: Alfred A. Knopf, Inc., 1984), especially 69-82, 147-79, and 213-17, where full documentation can be found. Here I have only cited direct quotations.

2. M[ary]L[yon], *Mount Holyoke Female Seminary,* South Hadley, Sept. 1835, 2. Copy in The Huntington Library, San Marino, California.

3. Quoted in Milo P. Jewett, "Origin of Vassar College," March 1879, typed copy, 6, Vassar College Library, Poughkeepsie, New York.

4. John M. Greene to Sophia Smith, April 28, 1869, quoted in Elizabeth Deering Hanscom and Helen French Green, *Sophia Smith and the Beginnings of Smith College* (Northampton: Smith College, 1926).

5. L. Clark Seelye, "The Need of a Collegiate Education for Women," paper read before the American Institute of Instruction, July 28, 1874 (n.p.: American Institute of Instruction, 1874), 14.

6. Ada Comstock, "Why Smith College Should House Its Students," *The Smith Alumnae Quarterly* 11 (Nov. 1919): 17.

HAMPSHIRE COLLEGE

The Making of a College, written in 1966 by future presidents Franklin Patterson and Charles R. Longsworth, formed the academic blueprint for Hampshire College. *Courtesy of the Hampshire College Archives.*

A Brave New World: Hampshire College

Charles R. Longsworth

President

The Colonial Williamsburg Foundation

HAMPSHIRE COLLEGE IS A BRAVE NEW WORLD in the sense that it turned the tables on many of the conventions of higher education, ventured into new ways of teaching and learning, the pursuit of which required courage, conviction, and persistence. Although outwardly flexible and apparently free-form, the college, as those of you who really know it understand, has a strongly shared set of premises, values, and standards for education, and a framework for demonstrating competence that belies the perceived disorderliness and reputation for complete freedom.

It is not easy, I find, to get back into Hampshire's founding. Aside from the passage of time and the dimmed memories, I find I have little need for the stimulation that came from those heady days and little capacity for reliving the sheer terror of many of the traumatic moments we endured as we tried to do what the cynics said wasn't needed and skeptics said couldn't be done.

Colonial Williamsburg, not without its challenges, allows one to deal with the world in a more orderly way and with a longer view. We have resources, and we have the stability and inertia that comes with long-time success — just the qualities, in part, that prompted the interest of the presidents of Amherst, Mount Holyoke, Smith, and the University of Massachusetts, unable to effect much change from within, in the creation of a new college in 1958, when *The New College Plan* was written.

To contribute Hampshire's short history — just twenty-one years of operation — to this series celebrating twenty-five years of Five Colleges, Inc., I'll try to relate how Hampshire came into being. This story may serve as a case study of the founding of an institution, though circumstances for each are unique. However, there are certain things that have to get done.

How does one of these long-lived things we call colleges or universities get started? We don't often think about that, just as we find visitors to Williamsburg haven't thought much about America as a British colonial possession. We think of Mount Holyoke as *being*, or America as *being*. But the life expectancy of colleges and universities in America is not good: hundreds came and went in the nineteenth century, our most prolific college-forming years, and those that survived seem to us to have been here *forever*. None of the local institutions was created within our memories. Smith, the youngest of the first four, was founded in 1875, the University of Massachusetts in 1863, Mount Holyoke 1837, and Amherst 1821. Hampshire opened in 1970, 95 years after Smith, 149 after Amherst.

We take our colleges for granted and do not always recall or even know their precarious early years. Amherst was so desperate in 1843 that faculty salaries were suspended. President Humphrey, with the agreement of incoming President Hitchcock, offered to share with the faculty at the end of the year whatever surplus there was. Amherst offered itself and its name twice in that period, once to Mr. Van Rensselaer and once to a Mr. Gray from Brookfield.

Hampshire College's twentieth anniversary, fall 1990. *Photo by Lionel Delevingne. Courtesy of Hampshire College Publications.*

Given this background, the high mortality rate of colleges, and general satisfaction with our known institutions, why would anyone want to create a new institution? Why not just give the money to one of the existing colleges (as I was asked several hundred times)?

Thus one might explain the skepticism that greeted Hampshire's beginnings and is evident still in this community and abroad in the world. Many people, even the early advocates, found starting a college outside the range of their imagination. I recall speaking in 1966 with Don Sheehan, the Smith faculty contributor to the New College proposal, to tell him that the new college was really going to happen. All he said was, "That's a hot one."

The skepticism, I suppose, also stems from an awareness of the financial difficulties of colleges today. Financial problems have brought down most of the new colleges. Hampshire is the sole survivor of the period in the 1960s when several experimental and experimenting colleges were founded. The others have disappeared or have been absorbed: Kirkland, absorbed by Hamilton; New College by the University of Florida; Eisenhower and Verrazano, closed; Florida Presbyterian, absorbed and renamed Eckert, after the drugstores. About the only survivor is publicly supported Evergreen in Washington State.

Further, Hampshire raises questions because it was and is hard to understand. It isn't a college like many of us know. No class attendance requirements, no credit hours, no intercollegiate athletics, no honorary degrees, no grades. Is that a college? But Hampshire isn't just absent the conventions and hence a formless blob. It has form, plan, structure, and philosophy. Despite the skepticism and the inevitable growth problems, Hampshire is with us, and twenty-one years later is graduating people who do good things well, and has a productive faculty and an established place in the Valley and the world.

Prior association with Hampshire often makes one a little suspect. When I am identified as a person who had something to do with Hampshire I am immediately offered (if the person has ever *heard* of Hampshire), "Oh, yes, that's the college in New Hampshire where students do whatever they want."

Sometimes, though, there are surprises. Sometimes the rewards are great.

General Robert E. Lee is the most revered figure in southern history. He is simply known as The General, just as those who went to Harvard think that it is The College. Lee, as you saw in Ken Burns's Civil War series, was indeed a fine and imposing man, and loyalty and respect are fully warranted. Lee's home, Stratford Hall, survives and is maintained and interpreted by the Stratford Hall Society, whose fiftieth birthday was celebrated in 1981. I was the speaker for the occasion. Stratford Hall sits on a promontory on the southeast shore of the Potomac River. It is a glorious site and the Sunday afternoon in 1981 could not have been prettier. At the appointed hour minus two minutes I was told I would be introduced by a woman whose daughter graduated from Hampshire. Ominous! She began with an accurate biography; then on to her daughter. She said, "Our daughter was not a good student in secondary school and was not promising college material. Hampshire saw something and took her. By graduation she was an intellectual cookie-monster, consuming knowledge at a great rate, and a convinced learner." What a relief!

Let's go to the beginning. In 1958 the presidents of Amherst, Charles W. Cole; Mount Holyoke, Dick Gettell; the University of Massachusetts, Jean Paul Mather; and Smith, Benjamin Wright, received a proposal from four faculty who had been asked to think about a new college design. The proposal, called *The New College Plan, A Proposal for a Major Departure in Higher Education,* was prepared at a time when imminent growth in the college-age population put demands upon American colleges and universities to provide space and opportunity for a vastly enlarged body of students.

That was the first reason for thinking about a new college. The existing colleges felt the pressure to grow and didn't want to. Charlie Cole told me that he thought Amherst (then a thousand; now 1,550) would lose its character.

Further, the presidents thought the existing institutions, working with a new college, might "develop new departures in educational methods and techniques."

That was the second reason. The presidents found their institutions resistant to change. They were successful, prestigious, conservative, and happy. Yet there were faculty and administrators and students who were restless, who thought there might be better ways to educate, that colleges could have a richer social life, that traditions should be challenged and broken. But these traditions were strong. As Dick Gettell of Mount Holyoke said in 1967, "We are not by definition schools that will run off at any new ideas." That was and is an accurate statement.

The four faculty persons who wrote *The New College Plan* were Caesar Barber, Amherst; Donald Sheehan, Smith; Stuart M. Stoke, Mount Holyoke; and Shannon McCune, University. In their letter of transmittal, they offered the hope we all share (and no self-respecting college catalogue could do without): "The most important contribution a college can make to its students is to develop in them a capacity to continue their education throughout their lives."

The New College Plan created a stir in higher education. It *was* a radical departure. It promised to unleash faculty initiative and student imagination — all on a balanced budget. The Ford Foundation, which had funded *The Plan* and related research through its Fund for the Advancement of Education, showed continuing interest to the extent of promising a grant of $6 million if the sponsoring institutions could raise a matching $6 million. Translated into today's dollars, the $6 million represents perhaps $18-20 million, a consequential sum. But, by coincidence, the presidencies of all the institutions except Mount Holyoke changed by 1961 and *The New College Plan* went on the shelf.

That is, except in the mind of Harold F. Johnson, Amherst College '18, who had followed the earlier developments with interest. Johnson, a Harvard attorney, partner of Coudert Brothers in Paris, military administrator in North Africa in World War II, and investing partner with fellow Amherst alumnus Charles Merrill in Merrill Lynch, was a shrewd investor who had accumulated a substantial fortune, much of which he wished to give away in a penultimate philanthropic gesture. His initial interest in Planned Parenthood was blunted by his assessment that the $6 million he was prepared to give was insufficient to make a difference in the world population problem.

Time passed and nothing happened. In December 1964 Johnson went to Charles Cole, the former Amherst president, to inquire as to any continuing interest in the new college idea. Cole in turn talked with Calvin Plimpton, then Amherst's president, reporting that Johnson

The farm owned by Robert and Cornelia Stiles formed the nucleus of the Hampshire College campus. This view is dated circa 1962. *Courtesy of the Hampshire College Archives.*

would probably give the needed $6 million start if the presidents of the Colleges and the University would support the development of the new college. Plimpton made the necessary inquiries among Presidents Mendenhall, Smith College; Lederle, University of Massachusetts; and Gettell, Mount Holyoke; and reported unanimous interest.

At the time I was Plimpton's assistant. In January 1965, he asked me if I would be interested in trying to develop the new college. I said I would and was invited to meet Mr. Johnson. He pronounced me fit.

I was intrigued by the challenge and was aware of the Amherst tradition of college founding. American University in Beirut was founded by an Amherst graduate. Amherst's President Hitchcock was the principal advocate of an agricultural college in Massachusetts and proposed an Amherst location so that Amherst College could cooperate with the new enterprise. Hitchcock also advised Mary Lyon in the founding of Mount Holyoke. More than one Amherst man served as president of Smith. One of the Smith presidents' relatives, Seelye Bixler, "refounded" Colby College by completing a new campus after Colby abandoned downtown Waterville, Maine.

The task of college founding has not been systematized. Colleges are founded only occasionally, and apparently none of the big consulting firms has found a fertile field in developing "college founding strategies." We proceeded by instinct and logic. In retrospect I have created a checklist of the tasks.

Get money

Select a site

Buy the land

Organize a legal entity

Get tax exemption

Find a leader

Get authority to grant degrees

Make an educational plan

Recruit key staff

Get more money — federal and foundation

Design and build a campus

Promote your ideas

Recruit a class

Open the doors

Run for cover

Get even more money

Get Money.   We had a huge advantage over all the other institutional upstarts of the 1960s in that Harold Johnson had promised $6 million and we had, we thought, the assurance of $6 million more from the Ford Foundation. While not enough to complete a college, $12 million in 1965 was a substantial sum, enough to assure that we would be taken seriously and thus be considered eligible for other support provided our ideas were sound and interesting.

With confidence that we really could proceed, I set out to select a site and buy land, Mr. Johnson having authorized $500,000 for that purpose.

Select a Site.   Initially, excited at the prospects, Polly (Longsworth) and I set out in our Saab in a blinding snowstorm, oblivious to the fact that the limited visibility precluded our making any intelligent judgments of the terrain and setting of the countryside over which we roamed, as we took in the four-college valley area as our own, available for a great new enterprise.

Good sense prevailed in due course and I did a "horseback" operations analysis to establish the target area that would locate Hampshire approximately equidistant from the three Colleges and the University. That resulted in a focus on the South Amherst area or the southeastern part of Hadley. Further exploration exposed a large undeveloped area, perhaps 1,800 acres, bounded by West Street, Bay Road, South Maple Street, and Moody Bridge Road. That it was split north-south by the Amherst-Hadley line made it a bit of a no-man's-land. It was almost entirely agricultural or woodland in 1965.

Picking a point in the midst of this tract turned out to be about three miles from Amherst College, five from the University, six from Smith, and seven from Mount Holyoke. Given the assumed likelihood that enough of this land could be purchased to make a campus, the location relative to the supporting neighbors seemed to be good enough to warrant asking Sasaki, Dawson and DeMay (now Sasaki Associates) of Watertown, Massachusetts, with whom we had begun conversations about campus design, to do a quick check of soils to see if we were going to be buying buildable land.

Initially, my assumption was that we should focus on Hadley because I doubted if Amherst would welcome yet another college, having already had its developable land diminished substantially by the holdings of the University and Amherst College. After confiding in Town Manager Allen Torrey (subsequently Hampshire's treasurer for sixteen years), I was assured that Amherst had not had its fill of colleges, and Hampshire would be welcome.

Buy the Land.   By the spring of 1965 I was a full-time land buyer. That was one of the great educational experiences of my young life. I was empowered and ignorant, a lethal combination. Who could I trust with my great secret — *we were going to start a college.* I thought hard and eventually turned to Winthrop (Toby) Saltonstall Dakin, an Amherst resident, town meeting moderator, Northampton attorney, and man of probity, wealth and discretion. I hardly knew Toby but I trusted him implicitly. So, to 39 Main Street in Northampton for the first of dozens of meetings with Toby Dakin.

Toby Dakin, Stan Teele, the Amherst College treasurer, and I developed a scheme which, if used today, would probably give the Amherst auditors gray hair, but it worked fine. When I could get agreement from a landowner to part with his land, I would immediately, on the spot, buy an option, giving him the appropriate form and a personal check. Then Stan Teele deposited Amherst College funds to my account, turning to Harold Johnson to forward money to make Amherst whole.

I began to wander about the countryside, calling on landowners. I tried various guises, all unsuccessful. Once, calling on the Warner family, farmers in Hadley, I dressed in my agrarian costume. We sat in their kitchen on Bay Road and discussed their dairy farm. Finally, one said, "And why do you want our land?" Before I could reply, another looked me up and down and said with disdain, "It's a cinch he's not going to farm it."

As the pattern developed it became obvious that the critically important land was a former dairy farm of 175 acres owned by Robert Stiles and his sister, Cornelia Montague. The farm had been in Stiles family hands since early in the century and was now marginally productive. The land was mostly open, with a few acres of woods. It rose to the west from West Street in South Amherst and had commanding views to the east and to the Holyoke mountain range to the south. Mr. Stiles and Mrs. Montague were in their sixties and lived modestly with a few cows still producing. In the course of poking around I learned that Roy Blair, an Amherst insurance man and classmate of Harold Johnson at Amherst College, was a trusted friend of Bob and Cornelia. So, I asked Roy if he would approach them with the proposal that we purchase their land with a life tenancy for them in the house (one of two on the property) then occupied by Mrs. Montague. Roy was not to disclose the identity of the purchasers or our purpose.

Roy did a masterful job. In the conversation, Cornelia tearfully recalled her and Bob's deceased brother Wayne, who had been a classics teacher in several southern preparatory schools. Cornelia said that Wayne had often expressed the hope that "one day there would be a school on this land." Roy replied, "I can't tell you what the buyers want to do with your land, but I can tell you that Wayne would be very happy." Bob and Cornelia agreed to sell.

There were other sellers and others who helped as did Roy Blair: J. Alfred Guest, then the alumni secretary of Amherst College, and George May, then the comptroller (and subsequently treasurer) of Amherst College, helped on a key piece. Howard Atkins, a major landowner and apple grower, owned the land adjacent to the Stiles farm, between it and Bay Road. He agreed to sell, and when I told him the purpose, lowered the price.

Andy Weneczek, a dairy farmer of Ukrainian descent ("I am not a Polack," he would say to me in our 5:00 A.M. sessions in his cow barn), was the holdout, but he, too, eventually sold with a life tenancy for him, his wife Stephie, and daughter Karen, and the promise of a job at Hampshire.

Andy, Bob Stiles, and Andy Dumbrowski, another farmer whose land we purchased, all came to work for Hampshire and were well-known and highly-regarded employees and friends of students and faculty.

As we purchased more land through the end of 1965 and into 1966, curiosity grew. We had not yet disclosed our purposes and now owned several hundred acres of land. One day I was in Amherst walking by the former Baptist church, since converted to real estate offices and a ticket office for the Peter Pan bus line. An acquaintance, one of the realtors, came out of the office and as we stood on the sidewalk put his arm around my shoulder. "Chuck, I think it's wonderful, just wonderful, what you're doing in South Amherst. Just wonderful for the town." I thanked him for his enthusiasm and support. Then he said, "Just what *are* you doing in South Amherst?"

Organize a Legal Entity. All during this period Toby Dakin continued to search titles and provide legal advice (we had organized a Massachusetts trust, The Trustees of Tinker Hill, to hold the land) and moral support. The burden to his law practice weighed on my conscience. I assumed he could afford to do as he chose, but I felt it was unfair that he should work so hard for the new college without reimbursement.

Finally, I told Toby that I was concerned and wanted to be charged for his services. I said, "Toby, I think this new college venture is a major distraction from your law practice." He replied, "Oh, anyone can practice law; this is making history!"

We had to form a corporation, recruit a board of trustees, get tax exemption so contributors could deduct the value of their gifts and we would be eligible for foundation and corporate grants, and we had to establish eligibility for federal funding. The Great Society programs of the mid-sixties were in full blush, there being a belief that higher education was one of the keys to the resolution of social ills, and we needed federal loans and grants to get our campus built.

How does a board get formed and get authority? It is a little like Dorothy in *The Wizard of Oz.* You just declare it to be so. Calvin Plimpton and I made a list, recruited the persons, and Toby Dakin, invoking the authority of the Commonwealth of Massachusetts, made the recruits into the Trustees of Hampshire College, succeeding the Hampshire College Educational Trust, which we had used as an interim organization after the Trustees of Tinker Hill blew its cover. Tax exemption was routine on application, and we were "in business."

Our quest for federal money was thwarted initially. We learned from Professor Livingston Hall, Roscoe Pound Professor of Jurisprudence at Harvard Law School, and secretary of Simon's Rock School, which he and his wife Betty Hall, former headmistress of Concord Academy, were founding, that there was no way a new institution in the Northeast could get federal funds. The criteria for federal funds eligibility were created by the various regional accrediting associations and the New England Association, the accrediting agency for the Northeast, had just two standards. An institution either was accredited, meaning it had been in operation for at least five years, had been inspected by a committee of educators and found fit; or was a candidate for accreditation, meaning that it had operated for at least a year and had a class enrolled.

The various accrediting associations forwarded the names of qualified institutions to a nice federal bureaucrat named Bertha Wilkins, who was the gatekeeper to federal funds. If you were on Bertha's list you could get money. If not, no funds. We met Bertha and learned all this firsthand.

After seeking help from Professor Ralph Burns, secretary of the New England Association, and a retired Dartmouth professor of education, we learned that some of the regional associations had created a new status, Correspondent of the Commission, specifically to help new institutions come into being. Initially, I thought that meant we had to have the capacity to correspond with Ralph Burns, but a trip to Hanover resulted in his ready agreement to try to persuade the keepers of the New England

Association to create such a status, provided he had some criteria in hand to help distinguish the qualified from the rest. He asked me to offer some criteria. As you might expect, I proposed criteria that Hampshire could satisfy, and subsequently, the Commission voted the new status and Hampshire was on Bertha's list.

As a result of our eligibility we immediately found funds to help plan the Johnson Library and, thereafter, construction grants for the library, the Cole Science Center, Patterson Hall, and three-percent loan funds for all of the Hampshire student housing and the dining commons. We also located our first librarian, Bob Taylor, who came for planning along with the grant, and developed friendships with two wonderful bureaucrats in the Department of Health, Education and Welfare, Jim Sullivan in the Boston office and Dick Ulf in Washington. Without their help and the expert grant and loan application and preparation by Ken Rosenthal, the Hampshire campus would not have been possible.

Find a Leader.   The presidential search was led by Charlie Cole and succeeded in relatively short order. Franklin Patterson, then the director of the Lincoln Filene Center at Tufts, was an experienced teacher and scholar, an educational innovator, and enthusiastic about the opportunity. He had a strong vision and lots of imagination. I introduced him to the new college by taking him in the snow up into Bob Stiles's pasture and telling him, "Here it is."

Pat, as he was called, was chosen in early 1966 to begin leading the college in June of that year.

Get Authority to Grant Degrees.   Meanwhile, to have the authority to grant degrees, institutional representatives had only to show that they were persons of experience and good character and a State agency could and did grant the authority. When Patterson and I and two secretaries sat in a farmhouse in South Amherst in 1966, we could grant any undergraduate or graduate degree except for an M.D. What a lost opportunity!

Charles Longsworth (left), second president of Hampshire, and Franklin Patterson, first president of Hampshire, at an early planning meeting. *Courtesy of the Hampshire College Archives.*

Make an Educational Plan. Franklin Patterson arrived in Amherst in the summer of 1966. He was fresh from a conversation with Edwin Land, the founder of Polaroid, who had asked Pat about his ideas for the new college. "You had better write it down," said Mr. Land. So Pat set out to write a book over the summer. The result was *The Making of a College: Plans for a New Departure in Higher Education.* As a starter he had *The New College Plan* and two other associated publications that reported research stimulated by *The New College Plan — More Power to Them: Experience in the Encouragement of Student Initiative,* and *Student Reaction to Study Facilities.* He also had a critique of *The New College Plan* drawn by Robert Birney, Amherst psychologist; Roger Holmes, Mount Holyoke philosopher; Fritz Ellert, University linguist; and Alice Dickinson, Smith mathematician. They formed a committee, chaired by Sydney Packard, a retired Smith historian and the first Four College coordinator. Each was asked to critique and extend *The New College Plan* by developing curricular ideas for the new college.

But Patterson really had the book within. His ideas and an amalgam of John Dewey, European university patterns, and his familiarity with and participation in curricular and teaching ideas of the sixties were the basis of the book. He created it in an incredible outpouring of energy in July and August of 1966, working most days from 3:00 or 4:00 A.M. until 5:00 or 6:00 P.M. By October we had a finished manuscript and an agreement for publication with the MIT Press. We arranged an accelerated manufacturing schedule and had the book in hand by December of 1966.

Recruit Key Staff.   It was apparent early on that we needed help. Pat hired Ruth Hammen, once a secretary to Stringfellow Barr, a colleague of Robert Hutchins at the University of Chicago and a founder of St. John's College, and I hired Virginia Aldrich, a South Amherst neighbor. Today Ruth is the senior employee of Hampshire College, with twenty-five years of service. Pat and I each found young lawyers to help with a variety of chores — he, David Matz, Harvard Law, and I, Ken Rosenthal, Yale Law. Ken had joined me a few years earlier in the conduct of a capital campaign for Amherst and I knew he was good.

Get More Money – Federal and Foundation.   Though we had secured access to federal money and had assurance of Harold Johnson's $6 million, my calculations of the capital requirements of a new campus and the deficits we would have to suffer until we reached a full planned enrollment of 1,300 students indicated that we had an urgent need for more fund-raising. Fortunately, Patterson was well thought of in the Ford/Carnegie/Sloan Foundation axis and was a persuasive spokesperson for Hampshire. We began to get some foundation support.

Further, and perhaps most important, we were counting on the support of the Ford Foundation's promised $6 million match of Harold Johnson's money.

We went to the Ford Foundation in the fall of 1966, armed with a promise and a plan. After deliberations that lasted until well into December we received the answer on December 12: nothing from the Ford Foundation. We reacted with incomprehension, then derision, anger, and, finally, determination to go ahead with Hampshire, Ford Foundation or not.

Charles Cole, as the senior advocate of the new college, went after McGeorge Bundy, then the Ford Foundation's president. Charlie argued that Foundation obligations extended beyond the tenure of Henry T. Heald, president at the time the promise was made, and that we had met the terms of the challenge extended in 1958.

Coincidentally, we tried another tack. Eugene Black, former president of the World Bank and a close friend of Harold Johnson, was, at the time, chairman of the Ford Foundation finance committee. Unknown to the Foundation staff, Johnson had Patterson and me meet Black at the River Club in New York to plead our case. Mr. Black, an imposing dignified Georgian in a double-breasted gray flannel suit, asked us a few questions, then rose and said, "Why, those fellows can't do this to you. You are bright-eyed and bushy-tailed. I'll call them." And he left the room. Pat looked at me, rolled his eyes, and extended his necktie like a noose, figuring we were cooked with the Ford Foundation staff for our endrun.

I don't know what ensued. There were no recriminations but we got only $3 million. This required another 2:1 match instead of accepting Johnson's money as the offset. In retrospect, that was probably a good thing in that we needed the money anyway, and the staff had probably calculated that it would reduce the risk of the Ford Foundation's wasting its money on an unlikely venture if it challenged us to raise more money to get theirs.

Design and Build a Campus. We engaged Sasaki, Dawson and DeMay to help with the campus concept and design, and Dick Galehouse, a young associate, led me through the steps necessary to include in *The Making of a College* descriptions, outline specifications, and preliminary budgets for a new college campus for 1,300 students.

Subsequently, several trustees, Patterson, and I, led by Harold Johnson, interviewed architects and settled on Hugh Stubbins Associates to begin the actual building designs while Sasaki completed the campus plan.

Construction of the first building, Merrill House, began in November 1968, directed by Howard Paul, newly hired from Turner Construction Company, and still the director of buildings and grounds at the college.

Keep Going – Promote Your Ideas. We thought we knew where we were headed and Hampshire had some good publicity, including front-page coverage in *The New York Times,* but the world in general did not know how we were planning to save it. Patterson went out on the hustings among the Four Colleges, whose faculty cooperation we needed, to the foundations and service clubs, and to influential individuals.

We began to appoint the first deans of the Hampshire schools: Everett Hafner for Science and Communications, Bob Birney (who came over from Amherst) for Social Science, Frank Smith for Humanities and Arts, and Dick Lyon as dean of the faculty. They helped with writings and school visits. Frank Smith, visiting a Des Moines, Iowa, high school in 1968, was astounded at the flock of students who had somehow gotten wind of Hampshire and turned out to learn more. The word was spreading.

Recruit a Class. We really didn't recruit the first Hampshire class. We simply accepted them. We accepted 252 of the several hundred first-year applicants and 250 came. This was rather vivid testimony to one of several possibilities. Hampshire sounded more interesting than other colleges. Other colleges sounded dull. Applicants were afraid they might not make it at the better-known competitive colleges. The applicants were suffering a surfeit of schooling and wanted to try an alternative that didn't look like more school, etc., etc. I suppose we'll never know. Students did tell us that they were attracted by the opportunity to progress by demonstrating competence rather than by completing class hours. Several said that if Hampshire had not accepted them, they were not going to college. Others, looking for a New Jerusalem, discovered that not even Hampshire could create a heaven on earth.

So, in September of 1970 Hampshire College opened its doors. Archibald MacLeish gave the opening address, saying, "We may be at a greater moment than we know." We were very nearly ready for the opening show, although Merrill House was absent finishing touches and some furniture. We were giddy with excitement, but faced rather formidable obstacles. We had to have new students, faculty, housing, and accompanying buildings ready each fall for the next five years if we were to have a chance to survive financially.

We built the faculty, the enrollment, and the buildings, and we survived. Twenty-one years later Hampshire has graduated 4,263 people. Its oldest living alumni are in their late thirties. The college now has 1,100 students, 35 buildings, a faculty of 96, and an endowment of just $10 million. Morale is high, excitement continues, and the fundamental ideas on which Hampshire was built are still in place. But Hampshire is still young and precarious.

Almost all who were associated with Hampshire from the beginning revealed an idealism about founding a college. Whether selling land (I wouldn't do this if it weren't for the new college, as Howard Atkins said) or building buildings (Don Shipman the Hadley plumber remarked one day, "I haven't been paid by the contractor but I don't want to let President Patterson down.") or coming to Hampshire as faculty and staff for less money, or in the case of Bob Birney, from a secure senior tenured

The Hampshire way of education: a student, the late Chris Lyon, and Professor of Design Earl O. Pope discuss an architectural project. *Courtesy of the Hampshire College Archives.*

position at Amherst, most displayed an idealism that was ennobling and enabling. Our faith in Hampshire as an idea was often shaken by the difficulties we encountered. Our faith was frequently restored by the wonderful human beings, highly educated and not so well educated, who joined in our belief that this was worth doing.

Has Hampshire fulfilled the dreams of its founders? In the 1962 study *More Power to Them: A Report of Faculty and Student Experience in the Encouragement of Student Initiative,* there is an introductory statement: "This report will describe one among several current projects aimed at countering the tendency of our undergraduates to leave too much of the initiative in their education in the hands of their teachers."

Assuming student initiative to be a good thing, has Hampshire encouraged it?

Here are quotations from a 1990 study of Hampshire by the Higher Education Research Institute at UCLA, one of the highly respected ongoing research efforts in higher education, the source of the freshman attitude studies you have seen for many years. "The major findings from the study of Hampshire College alumni suggest that the Hampshire experiment has been a very successful one. Early on, Hampshire had the vision to identify mechanisms through its structure and curriculum that encourage active learning — the kind of learning that is viewed today as one of the most essential ingredients in a successful undergraduate experience. We believe that Hampshire provides a model of active learning that can be emulated in many key respects by other institutions of higher education."

In several other ways Hampshire is different from colleges with which it is directly compared or which may be familiar to you. The following are relative statements summarizing the characteristics of Hampshire College graduates and comparing them with the graduates of a New England coeducational college of high quality:

- Hampshire has engaged nonscience students, especially women students who have avoided science, in the sciences and mathematics.

- Hampshire has encouraged and fostered growth in the capacity to work and think independently. This is frequently noted by graduates. Some who have experienced graduate school remark that they were not as well prepared factually as their contemporaries from other schools, but were better prepared in how to search and evaluate evidence, ask questions, and trust their own judgment.

- Hampshire graduates are more likely to pursue careers in public service, become entrepreneurs, participate in social and community organizations, and be involved in politics or civil rights, give money to causes in which they believe, etc. In other words to be active, involved citizens.

- Hampshire has developed a collaborative, learning faculty that is highly productive, and has "created a culture that is very supportive of the institution's mission to develop active learners with a strong social consciousness."

So there is evidence that the Hampshire College experiment is successful and has achieved a result that distinguishes it from other colleges.

There were disappointments. Bob Birney pointed to the largest in a recent conversation. It was a result of the naïveté with which we began Hampshire College. We really believed we could make a difference, not just in the lives of our graduates, but in the world. We thought that Hampshire, if successful, would, as Sandy and Helen Astin say in the Higher Education Research Institute report, "provide a model of active learning that can be emulated in many key respects by other institutions of higher education." Sadly, one thing institutions do not do is learn much from each other. The wheel is continuously reinvented. Dick Gettell was right, not in speaking about Mount Holyoke, but in general about colleges: "We are not by definition schools that will run off at any new ideas."

The difference today, as compared with twenty-five years ago, is in the more widely shared view of the value of independence of mind, of the usefulness of multidisciplinary study to understand complex problems, of the need for talent in socially important work, of the significance of the ongoing problem of injustice, of the failure of our institutions to teach science for citizens, of the waste when talented women avoid science, of the significance of new fields of knowledge, of new combinations of disciplines, of the changes in known fields, of the utility of technology in most fields! These are all issues Hampshire has addressed with some considerable success. Other institutions also are struggling with those issues. We need to share our new understandings. But sharing is offering and accepting. No institutions of any kind in this country have a worse case of the "not invented here" syndrome than have our colleges and universities. It is amazing how compartmentalized, provincial, and egocentric colleges can be.

Five College cooperation is a saving grace for its participants. There is a tradition of offering and accepting. Hampshire would not be were it not for Four- and now Five- College cooperation. And we would not have undertaken Hampshire with any optimism had not the promise of cooperation been explicit. Cooperation made it possible for Hampshire to attract the kinds of students and faculty who could do the work or qualify to teach in any of the institutions.

In spite of the disappointment over Hampshire's lack of broad impact, I can point to very real and important contributions Hampshire has made here in the Valley. Hampshire excels in teaching film and photography. Hampshire's contribution has made opportunities in those areas for Valley students as well as in fostering an understanding of the legitimacy of such study. Hampshire's leadership in library cooperation and technology application is clear. Hampshire is a leader in cognitive studies. Hampshire, in the words of the Amherst chairman, Tom Wyman, has helped democratize Amherst. Hampshire students have often injected a challenging skeptical voice in the classrooms of the other colleges.

Adele Simmons, third president of Hampshire, presents a diploma in the spring of 1988. *Photo by Lionel Delevingne. Courtesy of Hampshire College Publications.*

George Kateb, now at Princeton, and once one of Amherst's most challenging and popular teachers — and, I dare say, not an adherent of Hampshire's educational ideas — said to me one day in the mid-seventies, "Hampshire students are keeping me alive. This is a time in the cycle when Amherst students are somewhat too passive. The Hampshire students sit in the front row and challenge everything I say."

Hampshire's need for cooperation has created an urgency for interdependence to which the other institutions have responded generously, and in retrospect, to their individual and collective benefit. I have no doubt that the numbers and quality of applicants at the private colleges, and the quality of applicants at the University, is influenced positively by the rich opportunities Five College cooperation affords all students in the Valley.

Cooperation is needed more today than ever before, and not just by Hampshire. Each of the institutions faces educational and fiscal issues that can and are being addressed not only on the individual campuses, but through the shared enterprise that is Five Colleges, Inc. Hampshire is the most important and influential product of that cooperation, and despite cynicism and skepticism is a great achievement of the visionaries, primarily the New College Plan Committee, Harold Johnson and Franklin Patterson; and of the Colleges and University.

Franklin Patterson was the creator of Hampshire College. I think *The Making of a College* put it on the map and in the public's imagination. He was an effective promoter and fund-raiser. He was also a very private man. His real strength was in conceiving a plan for the college, firing it with his enthusiasm and idealism, and recruiting good people. He was less interested in building it or in its daily operation.

Adele Simmons, the third president, came when college populations were shrinking, Hampshire's applicant pool was shrinking, and the academic program, then seven years old, needed an overhaul. The college had been built physically and was on its feet but was in need of new energy, forward planning, and a broader base of support and interest. She gambled on deficit spending to maintain or strengthen standards, rebuilt the enrollment, and greatly enhanced Hampshire's education. Adele Simmons is a person of broad horizons, energy and determination, and considerable powers of persuasion.

Gregory Prince, the fourth president, brings a great deal of experience to Hampshire, is an old hand at academic administration (though a young man), has demonstrated his real understanding of Hampshire and a commitment to its values, and is working hard and successfully to build the college's financial resources and assure its future. His imagination and independence of mind will serve Hampshire well.

Hampshire was created by many people and many continue to contribute to Hampshire's success and to Five College cooperation. All of us who care about Hampshire thank all who have kept faith with Hampshire's vision and courage to experiment — who have appreciated its role in contributing to a diversified system of higher education, and who believe in Hampshire's future as a vital and integral part of the Connecticut Valley community of learning and teaching.

Groundbreaking for the first Hampshire academic building by (left to right): Franklin Patterson, Harold F. Johnson, Thomas Mendenhall (Smith), Calvin Plimpton (Amherst), John W. Lederle (University), and Richard Gettell (Mount Holyoke) on September 21, 1968. *Courtesy of the Hampshire College Archives.*

AFTERWORD

THIS IS AN ECLECTIC COLLECTION of essays. Each focuses on a different era and each tells a very different story. That the five institutions are in any way connected is barely perceptible until we read Charles Longsworth's eyewitness account of the founding of Hampshire College. Readers unfamiliar with Five Colleges, Inc., understandably might wonder what exactly it is that binds together either the book or the consortium.

To the initiated, to those familiar with the history of the individual institutions and with the development of cooperation among them, this collection makes eminent sense. It insists upon the individuality and idiosyncrasies of the culture on each campus and reflects the distinct legacies inherited by each, legacies which continue to inform and influence institutional behavior. In spite of occasional suspicions to the contrary, Five College cooperation thrives on these differences. Each college was, in fact, founded in order to provide a clear alternative to those institutions already flourishing in the hinterland of western Massachusetts.

Even Amherst, the oldest of the member institutions, came into being as a response to the limited choice in higher education then available to the "indigent young men of piety and talents" who lived in this part of the Connecticut River Valley. Before Amherst College existed as an option to them the only nearby choices were Williams and Harvard. According to historical accounts, the former was considered too far away and the latter too far out in its divergence from Christian orthodoxy.

Mount Holyoke provided a very different alternative — higher education for women. The University's founding as Massachusetts Agricultural College came at a time in our history when American higher education went public. The post-Civil War era and its encouragement of equal educational opportunities for women, including the same curriculum offered to men, was largely responsible for the creation of Smith College. It took almost a century more before a new cry would arise for yet another college in the Valley. Hampshire owes its existence to another era's challenge to the traditions and structures of the American academy.

One of the ties, then, that binds these five institutions together is the very reason each came into existence: to provide a different, distinctive alternative to the education offered at other institutions, even those already in the Valley. Those differences still prevail. Two of the private colleges remain all-women's colleges, an alternative to today's move toward coeducation. Even though Amherst did become coeducational it has not increased its student body significantly, insisting instead on keeping to its tradition of a small liberal arts school. Hampshire continues to offer an experimental approach to learning, with no grades, no departments, and no majors, focusing instead on the individual student's own course of multidisciplinary study. In spite of the vicissitudes of state support, the University maintains its commitment to graduate and professional training as well as to undergraduate liberal arts study.

Of course, it was no accident that these new alternative institutions of higher education were located in Amherst, Northampton, and South Hadley, some ten miles from each other. As Chuck Longsworth points out, Amherst College graduates and faculty actively participated in the founding of each of the other institutions. Some even joined the new administrations and faculties. How then does one answer the question: When did cooperation begin? In the 1830s, when President Hitchcock of Amherst supported Mary Lyon in her efforts to establish Mount Holyoke? Or in the 1950s, when the presidents of Amherst, Mount Holyoke, Smith, and the University appointed a committee to study the possibilities for cooperation? Or in 1965, when the institutions were formally incorporated, first as Four Colleges Inc., and later, after Hampshire's founding, Five Colleges? It is 1965 which we officially marked in 1990 when we celebrated the twenty-fifth anniversary of Five Colleges.

But althought it was the year in which the consortium was legally incorporated, 1965 marked more than the creation of a legal entity. By 1965 a significant amount of cooperation had already been accomplished: WFCR was established in 1960 as a Four College effort; a joint astronomy department was formed in 1963; publication of the monthly calender of events began in the early sixties; and a number of other projects were gestating, ready to be born. Incorporation gave a name to an existing and quickly maturing reality: Five College cooperation. In the last twenty-five years cooperation has grown and prospered. In 1967, the position of coordinator was converted to full-time, replacing the part-time faculty postion which had been in place for ten years. The staff of three has grown to twelve, and the one-room office to a separate building, the Five College Center.

Support for the consortium still comes in large part from the member institutions; but, added to that support is income from an endowment of over three million dollars and grant funds totaling in the millions each year. Five Colleges, Inc., is recognized nationally as a success in interinstitutional cooperation. We are applauded for the ease with which students cross-register for courses at the other campuses, at no additional fee; the ability to sustain joint departments and joint faculty appointments, even tenured ones; the tenacity to support a fare-free bus system; and the willingness at times to suspend institutional priorities for those of the consortium.

The institutions continue to support the consortium for the same reason that each was founded: to respond to evolving needs and demands made upon higher education by succeeding generations and different eras, while at the same time not eliminating the distinctiveness of each institution. Through the consortium the students and faculty have the best of many possible educational worlds. They can attend a small liberal arts college, but take courses at a university that offers the diversity size alone can afford. Or, as university students, they can experience a very different atmosphere on one of the college campuses. Although enrolled at all-women's colleges, students at Smith and Mount Holyoke sit in coeducational classes both on their campuses and at the other institutions. Hampshire students enjoy the opportunity to devise their own course of study while having open to them the chance to study within a more traditional environment. The University offers advanced students at all four colleges the opportunity to take courses at the graduate level. And graduate students at the University have a far greater choice of readers and advisors for their dissertations than would be available were the University not part of the consortium.

Cooperation also provides the faculties of each institution with a wider intellectual and professional community. The isolation specialists can feel on one campus is ameliorated by the presence of colleagues on the other campuses, with whom they often consult and collaborate in both their research and teaching. Like students, faculty members also enjoy the opportunity to inhale a different atmosphere.

The consortium, rather than melding the five institutions into one conglomerate, actually allows each to continue to honor its own traditions and individual missions, and still respond to the times we live in. It is hard, for example, for a small liberal arts college to offer every new field and every new specialty within a field. This is especially true today, when we are struggling to diversify our offerings, to acknowledge the need for an internationalized curriculum, without sacrificing the best of the past. When the institutions join forces they are able to increase both the range and depth of offerings from which students can choose. New fields like Peace and World Security Studies, Coastal and Marine Sciences, and Near Eastern Studies are intitiated as joint programs. Foreign languages can be introduced into the curriculum by sharing faculty. Chinese, Japanese, and Arabic were all first taught at the colleges in this way.

Throughout its short history, Five Colleges, Inc., has been suspect. "Kill it!" one of the first faculty coordinators was told by a colleague. Then as now, some fear the establishment of a sixth institution, one that will sap the strength and individuality of each of the five. And yet, as these essays so persuasively illustrate, each institution preserves its own personality and its own sense of history. The consortium helps by providing the flexibility to experiment with the new and by offering a wide range of different opportunities to both students and faculty without sacrificing institutional identity.

The celebratory year of 1990 has been followed by a year of planning for the future. Deans, faculty members, and administrative staff are all engaged in discussions of how the institutions can take fuller advantage of Five College cooperation in order to meet some of the challenges they now face. It is far too early to say what the specific results of these discussions will be. They are likely to include cooperation in adminstrative services and student services as well as in curricular offerings. What can be predicted is that we will probably do more together than we do now, that the consortium will continue to provide an opportunity for growth and change even in an era of fiscal constraint.

What can also be predicted is that Amherst, Hampshire, Mount Holyoke, and Smith Colleges and the University of Massachusetts at Amherst will survive as five distinct and autonomous members of the Five College consortium.

Lorna M. Peterson
Five College Coordinator

Contributors

Christopher Benfey teaches American literature at Mount Holyoke College. Among his works are *Emily Dickinson and the Problems of Others* and *The Double Life of Stephen Crane.*

Donald R. Friary is the executive director of Historic Deerfield, sponsor of the lecture series on which these essays were based. Friary holds a doctorate in American civilization from the University of Pennsylvania. He has written on early American history and lectured at Smith College.

Theodore P. Greene, emeritus professor at Amherst College, is the author of *America's Heroes: The Changing Models of Success in American Magazines* and the general editor of *Essays on Amherst's History.* He has also edited volumes on Roger Williams, Woodrow Wilson, and American imperialism.

Helen Lefkowitz Horowitz teaches American studies and history at Smith College. Besides *Alma Mater: Design and Experience in the Women's Colleges,* her works include *Culture & the City: Cultural Philanthropy in Chicago from the 1880s to 1917* and *Campus Life: Undergraduate Cultures from the End of the Eighteenth Century to the Present.*

Charles R. Longsworth holds degrees from Amherst College and Harvard University. He was an administrator at Amherst College before serving as the second president of Hampshire College from 1971 to 1977. He is currently president of the Colonial Williamsburg Foundation.

Lorna M. Peterson is the Coordinator of Five Colleges, Inc., the consortium of the five institutions discussed in this volume. Peterson holds a doctorate from Yale University and is an adjunct professor in the Slavic Studies department at the University of Massachusetts.

Ronald Story teaches history at the University of Massachusetts at Amherst. Among his books are *The Forging of an Aristocracy: Harvard and the Boston Upper Class, Generations of Americans, A More Perfect Union,* and *Sports in Massachusetts.* He is currently interim vice-president of the University of Massachusetts.